CONTENTS

For A' That

A Celebration of Burns

Gavin Wallace

A Spark o' Nature's fire

Shrove Tuesday, 1785. Robert Burns is hosting an evening's
carousing at Mossgiel Farm. In the midst of the craic,
Burns is arrested by a song in praise of married love by a
fellow Ayrshire farmer and poet, the sixty-year old John Lapraik.
So moved is Burns by its combination of sincere emotion
and *ingine* – genius – that he writes Lapraik a twenty-two
verse epistle, one of the less canonised of Burns' poems,
but undoubtedly one of his greatest. It begins:

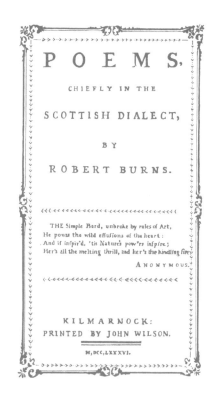

> While briers an' woodbines budding green,
> And Paitricks straichan loud at e'en,
> An' morning Poossie whiddan seen,
>   Inspire my Muse,
> This freedom, in an *unknown* frien'
>   I pray excuse.

> On Fasteneen we had a rockin,
> To ca' the crack and weave our stockin;
> And there was muckle fun and jokin,
>   Ye need na doubt;
> At length we had a hearty yokin,
>   At *sang about.*

> There was *ae sang,* amang the rest,
> Aboon them a' it pleas'd me best,
> That some kind husband had addrest
>   To some sweet wife:
> It thirl'd the heart-strings thro' the breast,
>   A' to the life.

Lapraik was an 'unknown' friend because he was absent and Burns had yet to meet him. In apologising for taking the liberty of writing to him and opening with a description of Burns' freedom to enjoy Nature and jovial conviviality, there is a deeply poignant irony: Lapraik had been forced to sell his farm as a result of a fiscal misfortune, and in 1785 was imprisoned for debt – horrors which would encroach closely upon Burns more than once.

In just a few lines, we have the three L's, the whole Burns DNA: the Land, Love, Liberty. Burns then goes on to compare Lapraik's art – in the affectionate but wry mock-heroic mode that is his very métier – to Pope and Steele, paradigms of the English Augustan refinement and poise to which he aspired, and to which his art was indebted. But what makes the 'Epistle to J. Lapraik' so great is not just the subtlety through which Burns' generous homage to a fellow vernacular poet provides a showcase for his own poetic genius. Its middle section sees an unexpected swing into a stinging attack on the stultifying pedantry of Academe, as opposed to the 'natural' inspiration of vernacular culture. It amounts to his entire political and aesthetic manifesto:

What's a' your jargon o' your Schools,
Your Latin names for horns an' stools;
If honest Nature made you *fools,*
    What sairs your Grammars?
Ye'd better taen up *spades* and *shools,*
    Or *knappin-hammers.*

A set o' dull, conceited Hashes,
Confuse their brains in *Colledge-classes!*
They *gang in* Stirks, and *come out* Asses,
    Plain truth to speak;
An' syne they think to climb Parnassus
    By dint o' Greek!

Gie me ae spark o' Nature's fire,
That's a' the learning I desire;
Then tho' I drudge thro' dub an' mire
    At pleugh or cart,
My Muse, tho' hamely in attire,
    May touch the heart.

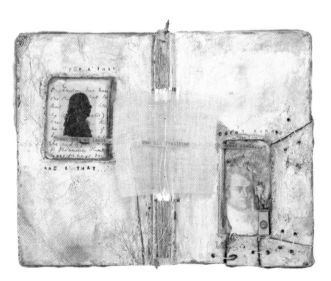

Robert Burns

This is a classic expression of the sly persona that Burns loved to inhabit, one which enjoyed encouraging others – especially so-called social superiors – to underestimate him when Burns, in fact, is already streets ahead in undermining the condescension. In this case, it is the enmired, 'uneducated' rustic who has already craftily disclosed he's as familiar with the 'correct' literary canon as your average graduate, let alone university professor. The 'Epistle to J. Lapraik' epitomises the genius through which Burns placed poetry, Enlightenment rationalism, and politics alongside religion on the cottar's mantelpiece, closing the schism between vernacular folk culture and sceptical abstraction; earthy _joie de vivre_ and intellectual discipline; the experiential and the theoretical.

Burns knew that understanding the balance between the experiential and the theoretical lies at the heart of understanding all great literature, whether academically taught or not. There is a delicious irony, then, 250 years on – which the author of the 'Epistle' would have relished – in the fact that within academia, two major developments can be traced in parallel in the first decade of the twenty-first century: first, Burns is only now beginning to recover from a long age of relative neglect (at best) and disdain (at worst) by academics and scholars; second, the formal teaching of creative writing at both graduate and postgraduate levels has become one of the most conspicuously successful and popular areas of the curriculum, particularly in Scotland. For A' That, a collection of new creative writing inspired by Burns, commissioned by the University of Dundee through its Creative Writing School, is a unique and happy conjoining of precisely those two phenomena, and the first publication of its kind by an academic institution.

A Homecoming, in more sense than one.

Two hundred and fifty years. Isn't that long enough, and hasn't 2009 in particular already seen enough, to see the wearing away of the guinea stamp of rank, for the gowd to be weighed and valued for its quality and not its formal markings, for our writers and specialists to have topped and tailed the final estimate of, to use Thomas Carlyle's words, 'what it was [Burns] really was and did'? Haven't we distilled, bottled, packaged and wrapped in enough tartan to stretch from Ayr to Adelaide and Dumfries to Darjeeling and back a thousand times our Scottish genie-genius? Is there really anything new for writers from Scotland and beyond to find in him? On the evidence of the sheer diversity, chutzpah and originality of the writing gathered here, the spirit of rantin, rovin' Robin is very much oot o' the bottle and on the loose again, assuming he was ever successfully captured in the first place.

For A' That is aptly named, for if there is one shared characteristic to be found in this extraordinarily eclectic collection of poetry, fiction and non-fiction, it is the urge to see, understand, and apprehend Burns as a subject as a whole, rather than to dwell on him – as commentators from just after his death until relatively recently have persisted in doing – as a bundle of fragmented and conflicting personae: Scottish nationalist, Hanoverian Bard, the Jacobin, the Jacobite, the International Socialist, drunken womaniser, prophet of free speech and free love, the radical revolutionary, the deferential Unionist. It is the multiplicity of Burns that is reflected here, a multiplicity which must inevitably contain opposition and conjunction, discord and harmony as all the greatest artists do, not necessarily as character blemishes, but as an integrity fit to reflect all the delights and tensions of life itself, a series of dualities capable of expressing all the contradictions of the age Burns lived in, and – just as importantly – the ages that have passed since his passing, and the age in which we live now. As radically different in style, tone and content as the pieces in this book are, one fact resounds throughout all of them: Burns is Our Contemporary. It's simple enough to test this before you read on. Think of the one iconic moment forever linked in the public consciousness with the

Opening Ceremony for the Scottish Parliament in 2004: Sheena Wellington leading the MSPs in singing 'A Man's a Man for a' That', in a ceremony which also included a specially commissioned poem, 'Open the Doors!' from the Poet for Scotland, Edwin Morgan, which was manifestly in the tradition of Burnsian scourging dissent. Or, fiddle with the historical dials and re-read the white-hot rage of 'A Parcel of Rogues' as a response to banking magnates filching millions in bonuses from the public purse following the recent near-collapse of the Western capitalist system, or the more recent MPs' expenses scandal. The results are, well, interesting.

It is above all Burns' generosity to his fellow writers, however, that is so amply reciprocated in the pages that follow. The poems by Jim Stewart and Jacqueline Thompson possess a beautifully understated nobility in honouring the profundity with which Burns dignified the hardship of peasant life in his work, while James Crossley's fictional miniature Red Rose transposes that context to a contemporary setting in an oblique and haunting fashion. And what of the 300-odd songs which have Burns' hand on them? In the radiant, razor-sharp lens of Janice Galloway's prose reminiscence, one of our greatest writers (and also a musician) lyrically illuminates just how far the songs of Robert Burns amount to a folk epic in themselves, the composition of which can be seen as a political act, a validation of folk experience in art, as well as an aesthetic triumph to set alongside the lieder of Schubert or Schumann. And how Burns would have 'thirled' at DBC Pierre's audacious parody of Burns and academia, where the 'Standard Habbie' meets post-structuralism: a wickedly inventive comic *tour-de-force* of counter-factual historicism which sees the fingerprint of Burns' influence in every major document of world culture from the Last Supper to the music of Mozart and the classical Latin poet Tibullus, with the Bard's last and greatest challenge against authority taken to the Vatican, no less.

There are other surprises. This is a collection which, partly by accident, partly by design, has invented a new literary sub-genre – Burns Statue or Memorial literature (as opposed to 'Burns' Stature' literature?) – from the easeful mastery of the great New Zealand poet Bill Manhire to the aching beauty of Kirsty Gunn's story Memorial, in which effigies of Burns dictate the content, narrative framing and emotional texture of the writing alike. In Ploughman's Naked Lunch by Stewart McCarthy and Christopher Whatley's thought-provoking essay on Burns and Dundee, Burns-on-the-plinth inspires two greatly contrasting interpretations on the infinite subject of Burnsian iconography, while a little-known memorial near Stonehaven to the poet's father is the starting-point for David Robb's Burns and the Longer View, a subtle reflection on Burns and time and place.

Whether your Burns Statue commemorates the Randy Burns, the Romantic Burns, or the Radical Burns, what this remarkable anthology confirms is how far every age has re-imagined and reinvented him in its own image, not least our own, in its attempt to seize that spark of Nature's fire and harness Burns' fierce, eternally blazing core of protean energy. For A' That is a salutary reminder of the danger for any generation of writers, commentators, biographers or hagiographers in believing that any act of newly 'unveiling' Burns means we can somehow 'finish' with him.

Robert Burns hasn't finished with us yet.

Dr Gavin Wallace is Head of Literature at the Scottish Arts Council. He has been active in many aspects of Scottish literature and culture as a teacher, lecturer, critic, journalist, editor and broadcaster at home and abroad and has co-edited critical works on Scottish Fiction and Theatre, and was a co-editor of the journal Edinburgh Review.

Janice Galloway

Singing for Suppers

"I don't know if you have a just idea of my character, but I wish you to see me as I am. – I am, as most people of my trade are, a strange wil o' wisp being; the victim too often of much imprudence and many follies. – My great constituent elements are Pride and Passion: the first I have endeavoured to humanize into integrity and honour; the last makes me a Devotee to the warmest degree of enthusiasm in Love, Religion or Friendship…"

Burns is, of course, a multitude. He was a man who took enormous care crafting his letters in Standard English yet whose best writings are in Ayrshire Scots; a man who enjoyed the crudest of crudery yet wrote the most heartbreakingly tender love lyrics in all literature; a sufferer from black depressions who loved company and every aspect of living, surviving blow after blow with resilience. Devout *and* rebellious; acutely aware of his lack of social standing *and* cocky; sure of his talent and apprehensive of his ability to succeed, Burns is not so much a mass of contradictions as a mass of unresolved emotions and drives.

That this rattle-bag of intellectual integrity, expedience, fear, ambition, loyalty and lust has become a national icon should come as no surprise. Burns, even more so than Byron, William Wallace, or even Mary, Queen of Scots, is rich pickings for interpretation, projection, transference. The People's Poet, perhaps: a King of Hearts with force of personality instead of a simper and heavy mascara. Repeatedly scent-marked as *ours*, he is idolised and excoriated, weighed and packaged for the temporary needs of Nation and individual alike. The dark horse who's candid to the point of offence; saturnine and genial, an infuriating shape-shifter and a stoic farm worker, we remodel him endlessly into what we most cherish, what we most suspect.

My Burns, the Burns of more than know it, is a song-writer. The songs are the strand of his work most of us know best, yet the work that academics acknowledge least. Folk song, passed down and altered over generations by *amateurs*, unverifiable and various, is un-canonical, not an area of expertise. Burns didn't care. Strapped for cash, with a full-time day job and the upkeep of more than enough children to pay for, he gathered and reworked the songs without fee or even accreditation, and this more than a century before Vaughan Williams, Kodaly or Bartok would do the same for the folk music of their own native lands. 'In the honest enthusiasm with which I embark in your undertaking, he wrote to one editor, to talk of money, wages, fee, hire, &c. would be downright Sodomy of Soul!'

Not all the tunes he wrote down as he travelled were Scottish and very few of them came with intact sets of words. So Burns rewrote the words, turning scraps into fuller, truer, more integrated visions. Taking for granted that the song culture of the people was high culture, open to all with no divisions, he reworked the melodies too, taking great care to retain their essence and marrying them to his new words indissolubly. A self-taught violinist who admired the work of Haydn and Mozart, his written music skills were more than adequate. More, he had fluency with what we might call the 'happiness' of a melody, its better flow; he could grasp the correct colour and arc of a tune to best fit it to meaning. And he did this with 368 songs.

This is no easy, *some-folk-have-it-and-some-don't* knack: this is practised artistry of the highest order certainly of equal worth to Burns' original poems. If we refuse to recognise that, valuing notionally 'original' creation as hierarchically superior, it is our sense of recognition that is at fault.

Of course, I didn't know that then. Then, a pre-teen during the sixties in post-Bard Ayrshire, my Burns was 1) local; and 2) who you did once a year for the school poetry competition whether you liked it or not. The verb 'do' is fitting, since he was not so much read as mumbled through or roared with odd inflections in front of whole-class assembly. A verse or two of half-understood 'To a Mountain Daisy' (served up as a ditty about a flower), 'Address to a Haggis' (served up as serious) or something in Lallans (my personal *bête noir* was 'The Puddock', a sub-Aesop fable that could easily serve as a Presbyterian sermon on the ever-present danger of thinking you were *it*) were standard fare. I remember tears and forgettings and trauma, teachers in ecstasies or despair at the fates of their favourites. But I do not remember much of meaning. There was a general pretence we just knew what was going on in the poems or that it didn't matter. Burns, like Shakespeare before him and to the same resentful effect, was shoddily taught, reduced, hog-tied, *compulsory*.

My 1970s teenage years, chirpier altogether, were governed by Ardrossan Academy. It was a 'good school', which meant you had to pass a *quali* to get there and Latin was thrown in as standard, and good it turned out to be. For all that, and unless *Macbeth* counts, I read nothing Scottish, at least not in class. But I sang folk songs and the music teacher took a shine to me, filling me with enthusiasm for performance. A voice, he pointed out, is the instrument we all carry inside. It's weightless, democratic and free. No initial outlay, no reeds or strings to buy; an instrument you could keep silent and still enjoy in your head for the beauty of its other half – the words.

I knew already that Burns did songs. Kenneth McKellar, a sweet-voiced, much underrated tenor, had been singing 'My Love is like a Red Red Rose' on Hogmanay shows for yonks, after all, but this context seems to have left me cold. Now, one of a handful of music students studying music with a wonderful, democratic teacher, I had better contexts altogether. Beside lute songs (and their love-affair with love-sickness); beside Schubert and Schumann *lieder* and Britten arrangements of the folk songs of the British Isles; beside Cumbrian dance music and Medieval English battle songs, Burns' songs appeared in a new light. Studying their notation added more: the physical shape, the movement and weave, the marked delicacy of phrasing. Huge leaps in the melodic line showed the mark of the fiddler – what's natural on a violin is often a brute for a voice. But his words, their clever marrying to the less easy-to-sing intervals, somehow managed to pull the whole together. Burns, with the skill of a sculptor, was carving new and living beauty into fallen, salvaged stone. What he also did, and beyond doubt, was add himself - those dashes of distinct personality and feeling that rise directly in Burns' letters and poems. They *speak*.

'Ca' the yowes', for example, one of the most haunting melodies I know, marries its odd, lonely line to faeries, birdsong, a shepherdess seduced half-sadly, infinitely tenderly, in a secret grove. 'Flow gently, Sweet Afton', ripples, like 'Die Forelle', with waves. Political songs, like 'A man's a man' with its martial air, easily accompanied by a snare drum heartbeat, sound inexorable as rhetoric, while 'Parcel o' Rogues' as tricked out modal as a Gaelic lament. There are funny songs (think of 'Rattlin Roarin

Willie's' tongue-twisting mouth-music), old ballads (like 'Tam Lin'), drinking songs for boisterous young men and boors and salacious mixed gatherings, tiny satires and the purple-tipped filth of 'The Merry Muses' (the best known of which, 'Nine inch will Please a Lady', is less explicit than most and is coupled with a demure wee tune as an extra joke). Then there is a whole raft of women, not just sung to or at or *about* by men, but speaking for themselves. The singer of 'Whistle and I'll Come Tae Ye My lad' is an arch and cheeky wide-eyed teen; 'The Lament of Mary, Queen of Scots' is sung by a world-weary woman whose sorry, lost life is over by middle-age. 'The White Cockade' is sprightly and light while 'Tam Glen' is heart-wrenching; 'The Gallant Weaver', a passionate declaration and defence of one woman's chosen *inamorato* while 'John Anderson' is sung by a clear-eyed yet wholly devoted wife. There are songs in the voices of snooty women and soppy women, besotted women and angry women, the shy and the dirty-minded, the strong and the weak: widows and mothers and reluctant brides. Two versions of 'Ca the Yowes' tell one a female and one a male version of the same encounter; different versions of 'Dainty Davie', 'John Anderson', 'Corn Rigs' (and others) have one or even two romantic settings and one or two that are rabidly lewd. Hook, line, sinker, I was caught.

Half way through my fourth year of secondary schooling, kitted out with a suitably uncontroversial selection of songs, I arrived at my first *bona fide* Burns Supper in a mini kilt and polo-neck. A friend of mine, a cellist with 20 inch flares, had been asked along as entertainment and hauled me, an *a capella* folk singer, along as part of the deal. Pay was involved and I was, understandably, thrilled. Even so, that first sally into the halls

of official Burns worship was a shock. The snug little performance space was in the middle of the gathering, all polished wood and whisky bottles and – I scanned slowly, grasping the unexpected fact – I was the only woman there. No barmaids, no waitresses, no lady to take the coats; just fifteen-year-old me and forty-odd older-than-me-by-a-long-chalk chaps. My face must have been a picture because the piper, due on stage, paused to buck me up. 'It's dead traditional here', he muttered. A man in a kilt was nudging him in the back with a haggis-loaded platter, keen for the off. The piper smiled, blew and bashed the tartan bag under his elbow in the guts. 'Sing nice and they'll no bite'. Live and learn, eh? Live and learn.

He was right on all counts. The haggis-stabbing cheered me up considerably but still, the evening had its jolts. The most uncomfortable part was certainly sitting through the fulsomely – delivered advice of a poem called 'The Henpecked Husband' ("Were such the wife had fallen to my part/ I'd break her spirit or I'd break her heart/I'd charm her with the magic of a switch/ I'd kiss her maids, and kick the perverse bitch"), especially since I had grown up in a household where smacking the wife around had not been an infrequent occurrence. Keenly aware of being the only potential *perverse bitch* in the room, I kept my eyes on the back of the hall, refusing to flinch despite the embarrassment, the confusion, the shock. These words were by the same man who had written the songs, weren't they? They were, they were. And so were the words of the 'Tam O'Shanter' poem that followed. And bits of the excruciating 'Toast to the Lassies' I squirmed my way through, longing for its close. And, indeed, all the rest. The songs I had chosen – one perfect love song, one

for a' that, and a'

it's coming yet for a

That man to man, the

shall brothers be for

THE SONG-WRITER

brave lament and 'There Came a Young Man', a woman's justified mockery of an arrogant wooer who makes a fool of himself by falling in a pile of dung, were his too. It was all grist, it had to be, but coping with this level of near-willful discordance was the work of years. It still is. Contradiction is sent to try us. It can be puzzling, intriguing or merely more to ponder, but it is not invalidation. Not in Life and certainly not in Art. I am still learning.

These days I no longer sing in public and wouldn't care if the whole tradition of the Supper fell into as much disrepair as the Spinning Jenny. What I've learned after years with and without them – and years of being a singing waitress too – is this.

The best of song is speech, one voice telling its truth. Burns knew this. He says so in his letters. He preferred clear, note-each syllables and simplicity of expression. He was, and is, a dramatist, a master of character and voice.

That he wrote songs from near-scratch and songs near-verbatim was no competitive enterprise. At no point did he ever see this work – collaboration in the widest sense – as less than his poetry. There is evidence to suggest that he felt in his bones that the songs, more than anything else of his output, would be what survived. What seems to have mattered to him was not entering a canon, but to offer a voice and make it *live*. That he was a creature of his time is unquestioned – no one, however far-seeing, can be anything else – but his voices are vital enough to chime authentically in the heart and mouth even now. As we fashion and refashion him, he refashioned words and music for us to do what we liked with. He's beyond caring what we think of him, if he ever did. What he'd prefer we care about is the work, its speaking to us. The songs.

Curiously, the man himself turned first to poetry – and song – at the same age I did. He was fifteen and the poem and song were one and the same: 'Handsome Nell'.

'For my own part I never had the least thought or inclination of turning poet till I got once heartily in love, and then rhyme & song were, in a manner, the spontaneous language of my heart'.

Burns' highly-tuned ability to speak the language of his heart, one-to-one and over centuries, is outstanding. The man's messy psyche, his erratic troubles, insecurities and ecstasies, his consistent questioning, defiance and trepidation, his long-term insights and short-term fears are legend. More than all of these, however, he is a song-writer, and a magnificent one. And that, on its own, is worth his celebration.

Janice Galloway was born in Saltcoats, Scotland and her acclaimed first novel, The Trick is To Keep Breathing (Minerva) won the MIND Book of the Year/Allen Lane Award and a Scottish Arts Council Book Award, and was shortlisted for the Whitbread First Novel Award. She is also the author of a further novel, two collections of short stories and her most recent book, a memoir, This Is Not About Me.

For my own part I never had the least thought or inclination of turning poet till I got once heartily in love, and then rhyme & song were, in a manner, the spontaneous language of my heart.

Robert Burns

Jacqueline Thompson

While we sing
The mouse and the louse
crawl between continents.
Holy hypocrisy spans centuries
as the cries of bastard weans
echo in the cities.
The mountain still springs daisies
as the Twa Dogs bite.
A face now stamps banknotes
where once only letters ran.
Through fluctuating fashions
he stood within the frame,
bowed head and bent knee
made meaningless, dulled to archaism
when poet and people are one.
This peasant did not kneel
and will never kneel while we sing.

*Jacqueline Thompson was born in Arbroath
and currently lives in Dundee. She graduated
from Dundee University in 2009 and will
begin an MLitt in English Studies there in
September 2009. She has had her work
published in New Writing Dundee.*

Robert Burns

From 'to J. S****'

Just now I've taen the fit o' rhyme,
My barmie noddle's working prime,
My fancy yerket up sublime
               Wi' hasty summon:
Hae ye a leisure-moment's time
                  To hear what's comin?

Some rhyme a neebor's name to lash;
Some rhyme (vain thought!) for needfu' cash;
Some rhyme to court the countra clash,
               An' raise a din;
For me, an *aim* I never fash;
             I rhyme for *fun*.

The star that rules my luckless lot,
Has fated me the russet coat,
An' damn'd my fortune to the groat;
               But, in requit,
Has blest me with a *random-shot*
             O' countra wit.

Bill Manhire

The Best Burns Statue

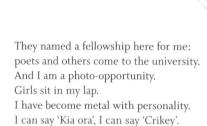

I am the best Burns statue.
In fact, there are four of me.
The first was in New York, Central Park.
Another is in London city.
There is also the one in Dundee.
But I am the best Burns statue.

We are men of identical bronze.
Sir John Steell cast us in pieces.
We all inhabit our stumps.
There is one stump to sit on
and another for resting the arm
while one thinks about poetry.

They say I am composing 'To Mary in Heaven'
and gazing at the Evening Star.
But the Otago Harbour is all that I can see:
ships at anchor, and then the Peninsula
with its edges of dusk and sand.
Then South America.

Yes, I am the best Burns statue.
I sailed 12,000 miles across the sea
to be here in Dunedin, my back
to the kirk and facing the pub,
and the Town Hall just to the left of me.
I am the poet of freedom and humanity.

I am single yet made of many parts.
I still have my chisel marks.
Come close and you can see. In 1887
my own great grand-niece unveiled me
before 8,000 folk in a fine assembly.
Oh I am the best Burns statue.

They named a fellowship here for me:
poets and others come to the university.
And I am a photo-opportunity.
Girls sit in my lap.
I have become metal with personality.
I can say 'Kia ora', I can say 'Crikey'.

All four of us are fine in full-face or in profile;
nine feet high, with impressive heads of hair.
I was myself a millennial project quite recently.
For ten weeks a company called CARE
repatinated me. The dirt was gone,
they gave me back my quill.

Hence I may now reach again for the scroll
lying out there in front of me . . .
see how it trembles in the wind from the sea!
And that reminds me of a further reason why
I am the best Burns statue: not one
of those others has the Southern Sea . . .

yet I would have quite liked
the wee dog, or the daisy.

Bill Manhire is an award-winning New Zealand poet, short story writer, and professor. Bill was New Zealand's inaugural Te Mata Estate Poet Laureate, and is a four-time winner of the New Zealand Book Award for poetry. He currently lectures in English and creative writing at Victoria University of Wellington, where he is also the director of the International Institute of Modern Letters.

DBC Pierre

UNIVERSITY
OF DUNDEE
ARCHIVE/ITEM
3(B):NOTE

THE SUPPRESSION AND UNDERVALUATION IN SCOTLAND
OF ROBERT BURNS DUE TO HISTORICAL OMISSION AND
MANIPULATION

*Extract from an introduction to the Doctoral dissertation by Darius
Bartholomew Constable Pierre, University of Dundee, Scotland, 2009.*

Background:

The first signs seemed like a joke. On 28th of March 1989 a
student journal[1] from Uppsala University in Sweden claimed
that lyrics to an obscure Finnish tango[2], if translated into Turkish,
recorded, and played backwards, rendered the following verse:

My blessin's upon thy sweet wee lippie!
My blessin's upon thy e'e-brie!
Thy smiles are sae like my blythe sodger laddie,
Thou's aye the dearer, and dearer to me!

But I'll big a bow'r on yon bonie banks,
Whare Tay rins wimplin' by sae clear;
An' I'll cleed thee in the tartan sae fine,
And mak thee a man like thy daddie dear.

Moreover the journal claimed that regardless of who read the
translation, and even if they understood no English, the verse
manifested in an authentic eighteenth-century Scottish brogue.
Of course such a farcical entry in an obscure student's periodical
warranted – and received – scant attention or endorsement.
But in 1992 the recording itself was certified by independent
linguists from Ankara and Manchester, and circulated to certain
faculty members at Uppsala. So improbable was its occurrence
that the then-associate professor of English, Johannes Kjeldsen,
quietly set about replicating the result in a double-blind
experiment with translators and audio engineers chosen

at random. The result was the same. A select multi-disciplinary
crew of experts was let in on the finding, and after two feverish
years, on the 10th November 1994, Kjeldsen delivered the
announcement which exposed him to widespread ridicule among
Burns scholars; he confirmed that the recording was a word-
perfect rendition of the entire Robert Burns song of 1787,
Bonie Dundee[3], stating moreover that it was in Burns' own voice.

What infinitesimal chance would govern such an occurrence by
coincidence? How otherwise could the recording be explained?
Vexatious questions remained to be answered, and the professor
duly took a cautious stance. On a summer break the following
year, he loaded his trunks and travelled by steamer to Dundee,
where the bard was famously born in a university robing-room,
and where he spent all his youth pursuing scholarship in physics,
art, astronomy, medicine, plus a new discipline – economics – led
by his Scottish contemporary, the somnambulant and suspected
simpleton Adam Smith. It was here, two centuries later, in the
university's vast archive, that Burns' personal correspondence
offered Kjeldsen tantalising new clues. In a note from W.A.
Mozart thanking the bard for advice on the arrangement of a first
flute concerte[4], the composer mentions a garden party in Vienna
which the two had earlier attended in the company of J.W. von
Goethe and his visiting great-niece Clara Schumann. Here, after
some abundance of refreshment, a quip by Emanuel Swedenborg
that Turks and the Dutch must surely have their own heaven,
prompted a reference by Burns to the 'Byzantines' present at the
gathering – the first recorded instance of his having contact with
Turks. The second instance appeared in a letter[5] from Burns to
the Comtesse D'Aubray some years later, after his heroic defeats
in West Prussia and Schleswig-Holstein led to the collapse of
their marriage: in the letter Burns recounts an exchange with
the young Joseph Stalin in which they voice concerns about
the emerging Ottoman empire. Over the typewritten word
'Ottoman' Burns has scrawled in ink: 'Scunners.'

While falling short of absolute answers these leads were compelling enough to propel the professor eastwards where a discovery awaited him which, if released into the public domain, would shake the very foundations of Scottish national identity. Arriving in Damascus by caravan, Kjeldsen was met by classical scholar and chemist Cayman Al-Masri, who presented an archaeological find which eclipsed the recording in its significance. During excavations for an immigration bunker in Sardinia a text had been found which appeared to be an unknown set of notes and sketches by the classical Latin poet Albius Tibullus. In it, the following verse appeared:

On that place over there lives a girl;
Could I describe her shape and style;
She is far better than our girls,
With her two sparkling eyes that defile.

She's sweeter than the morning dawn,
When rising Phoebus first gives glimpse,
And dew-drops twinkle o'er the lawn;
Her sparkling eyes flash hot like imps'.

She's stately like yon Afghan hash,
That grows layers of nubile sheen,
And drinks the stream with vigour brash;
Like her eyes drink all between.

The fragment had already been studied at Port Said university by the time of Kjeldsen's arrival, even though scholars at Port Said were not part of the Burns investigation, nor could they have the least reason to suspect a Burns connection with the classical text. Still the verses rang a bell for one of them, whose interest was particularly drawn to this note in a second hand which appeared beneath Tibullus' words:

'I'd put Cessnock Banks, Tibbie, for the lassie. Cessnock Banks and roguish een, there's ma good lad.'

Thermo-luminescent procedures dated both scripts to the century before Christ. Then Al-Masri used computer matching to arrive at the following startling counterpart attributed to Burns himself nearly eighteen centuries later:

On Cessnock banks a lassie dwells;
Could I describe her shape and mein;
Our lasses a' she far excels,
An' she has twa sparkling roguish een.

She's sweeter than the morning dawn,
When rising Phoebus first is seen,
And dew-drops twinkle o'er the lawn;
An' she has twa sparkling roguish een.

She's stately like yon youthful ash,
That grows the cowslip braes between,
And drinks the stream with vigour fresh;
An' she has twa sparkling roguish een.

Such was the astonishment of this finding that, in a move unprecedented anywhere in the academic world, funding was granted to the scholars to simply close their files for six months and recoil. But it is the nature of great secrets to escape, as the impact of their news is too weighty for a single consciousness to bear. In the case of the Burns mystery this escape immediately took on teeming proportions, travelling like the draught of a blaze through the narrower corridors of academia, where obsessives of every discipline began matching all written material against Burns' known works. Original tablets, papyruses, vellums and papers were decanted and checked again for evidence of a second hand.

University
Room...

Dear Esteemed Comtesse,

It is incumbent upon me to intimate to that gentle and good self, despite – nay, even because of our altered relationship – the unfavourable circumstances we currently find ourselves in, that I have, once again, been in contact with the Turks.

Through my recent acquaintance – a most eager friend, I believe – as well as through my own unfortunate experience at the hands of that empire, referred to as _scunners_, I have both felt a change of opinion, both in myself and in others in this respect. This esteemed acquaintance is one Joseph Stalin (and a very fine young man he is, too, if a little unyielding in his convictions at times). In this particular instance, however, I admit to total concurrence with that opinion.

I trust that you have enjoyed the arrival of this letter – written on what is called a typewriter, no less – as much as I have enjoyed the act of writing it. Please excuse the small errors, which must be put down to a lack of familiarity with the specific techniques that must necessarily be acquired in the mastering of this wonderful new machine.

Yours as ever,

Robt Burns

Within four days the switchboard in Damascus was alight. Three discoveries from Rome, a dozen from Constantinople, and from Leipzig an indication of more substantial feelings between Burns and Tibullus than those of simple mentor and pupil, as evidenced in this original of a work long merely associated with Strathspey:

O Tibbie, I hae seen the day,
Ye wadna been sae shy;
For laik o' gear ye lightly me,
But, trowth, I care na by.

Yestreen I met you on the moor,
Ye spak na, but gaed by like stour;
Ye geck at me because I'm poor,
But fient a hair care I.
O Tibbie, I hae seen the day, &c.

When coming hame on Sunday last,
Upon the road as I cam past,
Ye snufft and ga'e your head a cast-
But trowth I care't na by.
O Tibbie, I hae seen the day, &c.

I doubt na, lass, but ye may think,
Because ye hae the name o' clink,
That ye can please me at a wink,
Whene'er ye like to try.
O Tibbie, I hae seen the day, &c.

But sorrow tak' him that's sae mean,
Altho' his pouch o' coin were clean,
Wha follows ony saucy quean,
That looks sae proud and high.
O Tibbie, I hae seen the day, &c.

Altho' a lad were e'er sae smart,
If that he want the yellow dirt,
Ye'll cast your head anither airt,
And answer him fu' dry.
O Tibbie, I hae seen the day, &c.

But, if he hae the name o' gear,
Ye'll fasten to him like a brier,
Tho' hardly he, for sense or lear,
Be better than the kye.
O Tibbie, I hae seen the day, &c.

But, Tibbie, lass, tak' my advice:
Your daddie's gear maks you sae nice;
The deil a ane wad speir your price,
Were ye as poor as I.
O Tibbie, I hae seen the day, &c.

There lives a lass beside yon park,
I'd rather hae her in her sark,
Than you wi' a' your thousand mark;
That gars you look sae high.
O Tibbie, I hae seen the day, &c.

And this was not all.

In March 1995 a message arrived by hand from a Cardinal Taekema, then in charge of the Vatican's highly guarded Papal archive. Opening the message was to prove the beginning of the end for Kjeldsen's research. In strictest secrecy, the cardinal invited him to a suite at the Hotel Raphael in Rome, where he showed the professor copies of biblical and pre-biblical originals never seen outside the Papal circle. The first of these was an early draft of the first psalm:

On that place over there lives a girl;
Could I describe her shape and style;
She is far better than our girls,
With her two sparkling eyes that d...

She's sweeter than the morning dawn,
When rising Phoebus first is seen climbs,
And dew-drops twinkle o'er the lawn;
Her sparkling eyes filled hot like dime...

She's stately like yon Urown bush,
That grows langous of noble sheen,
And drinks the stream with vigour brush...
Like her eyes drink till se'en.

I'd ... Cessnock Banks ti bbre...
lass... Cessnock Banks and ung nosh
there's ma good la...

The man, in life wherever plac'd,
Hath happiness in store,
Who walks not in the wicked's way,
Nor learns their guilty lore!

Nor from the seat of scornful pride
Casts forth his eyes abroad,
But with humility and awe
Still walks before his God.

That man shall flourish like the trees,
Which by the streamlets grow;
The fruitful top is spread on high,
And firm the root below.

But he whose blossom buds in guilt
Shall to the ground be cast,
And, like the rootless stubble, tost
Before the sweeping blast.

For why? that God the good adore,
Hath giv'n them peace and rest,
But hath decreed that wicked men
Shall ne'er be truly blest.

Next, however, the cardinal produced a document that carried behind it all the fearsome weight which the Vatican and its worldwide legions of followers could muster; a weight now turned to the suppression of any further Burns research.

It was a sketch, with notes, attributed to the apostle Paul at the Last Supper itself. In the sketch, a thirteenth figure appears beside the Nazarene – indeed he occupies the very centre of the table, and all present are turned to him agog. A quotation appears in an uncertain hand below the drawing:

Let other poets raise a fracas
'Bout vines, an' wines, an' drucken Bacchus,
An' crabbit names an' stories wrack us,
An' grate our lug:
I sing the juice Scotch bear can mak us,
In glass or jug.

EPILOGUE TO THE DISSERTATION:

Once the meeting with the cardinal was over, every document, expert, artefact or research paper from Kjeldsen's quest evaporated without trace or explanation, just as quickly as they had all appeared. Moreover this happened precisely as the world of scholarship awaited with bated breath the proofs of his wild assertions. Kjeldsen was socially and professionally ruined. For a time between 1996 and 1999 he took to the pen himself, and ran with the Scottish poets. He inspired sufficient comradeship in these that, as he lay in a Glasgow tenement consumed by his loss and by strong drink, the Scottish poets mounted a final challenge to the Vatican. A small congress was eventually mounted by the Holy See to be seen to dispense with the matter once and for all. And from it – which was the last ever heard on the matter, given the church's mighty powers – this anecdotal account of a final exchange between Scottish poet and clergy:

'My son, you were bound to lose – you have no structure, no hierarchy.'

'Truth dis nae need a structure,' replied the poet.

'But there is no power invested in you – you carry only the power of your self, and your loose association with others of your kind. Whereas look, look at this,' the cardinal beckoned a passing student priest, '– soon he will be a priest, and have invested in him all the devotion of a flock of souls. Then he might become a

£150 £3 per Cent. *Annuity*, 1744.

RECEIVED ... Last of *March*, 179...

Let ... fools raise a fracas
'Bout ... wines, an' drucken Bacc...
... stories wrack us,
... lug ...
... Scotch Dear, can mak us,
In glass or jug.

Interest or Share in the ... Joint Stock, erected by an Act of Parliament of the Seventeenth Year of the Reign of his Majesty George II. intituled, An Act for raising by Annuities ... Lottery, ... mentioned, the Sum of One ... Pounds, at Three Pounds ... of the Year Seven ... this Day transferred to ...

... as my Hand ...

£149 12 6
... 3 9
£149 16 3

cardinal, and have invested in him the faith of many flocks, many priests. Or he might become a bishop, and speak for whole cities of souls. You see?'

'An' then wha'?' scoffed the poet.

'Well. Conceivably I suppose he could become pope.'

'An' then wha'?'

At this the cardinal is said to have thrown down his hands and shaken his head, exasperated: 'Look, what more do you want – that he becomes God?'

And the poet sniffed, and before turning for haim, said:
'One o' our lads did it.'

[1] Upps Gamla Smorgasbladet, Volume I, No. 3, p.14

[2] Elsa, Kohtalon Lapsi

[3] Of course the word Bonie in the title of Burns's song has universally been taken as an earlier spelling of Bonnie, but this is not so, as a note from Burns himself confirms. The word he used was Bony, referring to Dundee's stark, skeletal condition in the wake of simultaneous and prolonged attacks across the Tay from both France and Prussia, the latter of which occupied Tayport and Leuchars for nearly six years leading up to Dundee's victory, and the subsequent signing of the Fife Treaty in 1896. As Burns later quipped: 'There's nane'll tak the wee auf mein bonie auld Dundee.'

[4] Wolfgang Amadeus Mozart Flute Concerto No. 1, K.313

[5] Anecdotally one of the first ever typewritten letters, posted within months of Burns' invention of the autodigitary letter-uichter, or typewriter.

DBC Pierre was born in 1961 in Reynella, Australia. He was brought up in Mexico and the UK, and now lives in Ireland. His debut novel, Vernon God Little was the winner of the 2003 Man Booker Prize for Fiction. His second novel, Ludmila's Broken English, was published in 2006.

...the man, in the place where...
...hath happiness in stor...
...though I'm not... that...
...nor lean... around...

...or from the seas of...
...eth forth his eyes...
...nt with humility and...
...full walks before...

...man shall flourish...
...which by the streamle...
...fruitful top is...
...firm the root bel...

...but the... blossom...
...fall to the ground...
...like the root...
...before the sweeping...

...for why? that God th...
...hath giv'n them pea...
...but hath decreed tha...
...shall ne'er be...

Robert Burns

The Lament

Ye winged Hours that o'er us past,
    Enraptur'd more, the more, enjoy'd
Your dear remembrance in my breast
    My fondly-treasur'd thoughts employ'd.
That breast, how dreary now, and void,
    For her too scanty once of room!
Ev'n ev'ry *ray* of *Hope* destroy'd,
    And not a *Wish* to gild the gloom!

Kirsty Gunn

Memorial

Not that she would ever put it this way, let alone turn it into something that might read like a story, but the fact is, when she starts thinking around the two events that seemed to mark the beginning and the end of her marriage, what she sees is one statue at one side and another at the other. Like bookends, is what the image is. And her life with Karl, those thirteen years in between when she was with him, like titles of books facing out of the shelf but she hadn't read any of them. All that time she'd never even looked inside.

And the statues were identical. Is how she remembers it, anyway, looking back. The same dead poet up on his box in the middle of a hot winter's day surrounded by foreign birdsong and strange trees as the one on the grey hill in the Borders that last weekend, after Karl had told her about his affair and how long it had been going on. He was still seeing her, he'd said, the woman he was involved with, but couldn't they make a go of things anyway? Because they were best friends, after all, him and her, they'd been like that since they met. And they liked doing the same things, didn't they, and wasn't that the most important part of marriage? To have interests in common? Isn't that what, Karl had said, kept people together in the end?

Like walking. That was how they'd met, at the University Rambling Club, and so quickly fell into the routine of going out to the hills in the weekends, coming back late or sometimes taking a tent with them in the summer months and staying out overnight. There was that exhaustion of lying down in their sleeping bags at the end of a long day and she can see now how that could have easily felt like deep contentment, happiness even. No wonder then he'd quickly called it love, Karl had, and she'd believed him. She'd ended up believing it for a long time.

Even that day when they were out in the Borders, after he'd told her about the woman he'd met who worked at the library and

about all the time they'd had together and that he couldn't keep it secret any longer because he wasn't that kind of man … Elisabeth had not exactly realised at the minute of his confession that she would leave him as a result of it. For there it was still between them, the pleasure of the landscape, the miles they'd already come. She'd looked around her, from her place on the hill, taking in the lovely silence and the quality of the air, and yes the words Karl had said were there, but so too was the knowledge of the thermos in his rucksack, the delicious sandwiches she'd made that morning in hers … And nothing else had seemed as real as that, had it? The routine of their life together, it's childless, contented pleasures? She'd even said to him, hadn't she, as they'd stopped on the side of that hill and she'd looked all around her at the great bare expanse of wintry brown and grey … 'I think I understand what you mean …'

But then they'd walked on, and that's when she'd seen that the mark on the landscape that she'd noticed when they stopped, that she'd thought was some kind of cairn or obelisk, was actually the statue of Robbie Burns, and the same one – that other a copy of this perhaps – as the statue she'd seen all those years ago, on that holiday when Karl had asked her to marry him.

That holiday. You could say it had been like another part of their friendship too. That summer after they'd both graduated and they'd booked plane tickets straight away, making lists of what they'd need to take, walks they'd plan, with Karl organising every little detail… He'd made sure he could find the cheapest deal for one of those long-haul flights where you stop off everywhere in the world – the US and India. The Far East and Australia all the way to New Zealand and then home. He'd said it would be their big adventure, 'OE' they called it 'Down Under' meaning 'Overseas Experience' – like all the kids from New Zealand and Australia came through to Scotland for a year. Only this would be them having the adventure, leaving one side of the world for

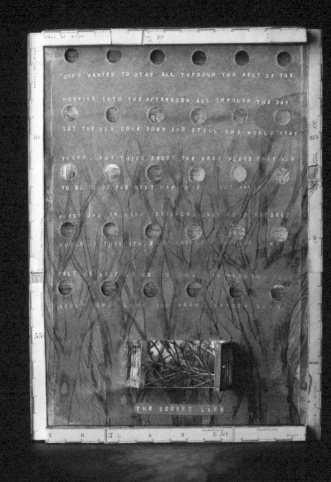

another, with nothing but their backpacks and their walking gear, all the money they'd saved, and, somewhere tucked into the corner of one of Karl's pockets, a tiny diamond ring.

Karl had told her, when they'd got home again, that he'd always planned for it to be in New Zealand when he would ask her to marry him, as far away as they could be, so that, as he put it 'There'd be no going back.' Only look at him, Elisabeth had thought that day in the Borders as they'd got closer to the statue and she realised it was the same one: he had gone back on his word after all. He'd gone right back. Though perhaps, she thinks now, in another way, he'd only gone back to being the same 22- year-old he'd been when he'd said it was her he wanted to be with all the time, sleeping with a young woman every night and waking holding her tightly in his arms like he's afraid she'll disengage herself from him in the dark, that she'll quietly ease out one shoulder and arm from the circle of his embrace and get away before he sees her go out the door … Only that young woman was no longer Elisabeth. It was someone else.

And that was when, when she'd come upon that statue, something stirred in her then. But not because of him. Not the sight of the dead poet up there on his plinth or whatever it was called, with the dates of his birth and his death and some half worn out bits of his poems beneath his iron feet … It was something else, the memory of another day with another statue, long ago, and of a sensation that she'd had then in the pit of her belly, ever since Karl had given her the ring, like a little nub of hardness. Like she'd swallowed the ring, been made to swallow it. That Karl had not just put it on her finger like he'd done on some beach somewhere in the North Island but had tilted back her head and poked it right down her throat like she was an animal and it was a pill.

For that's what she'd been thinking about the morning of that other statue. How being married felt like something she'd had to swallow. Though he'd asked her in a perfectly ordinary way and she'd said yes and now here they were in a different part of the country anyway and having a row about directions because she'd been driving the hire car and he'd slept with the map on his knee

and she hadn't woken to ask him which way when the road had taken a fork around the base of that big mountain, what was it called, where they were supposed to be joining a walk that was setting off the following week … Still it had continued to sit with her, the feeling of the little nub of Karl's will, sitting there in the pit of her and not dissolving.

He'd been cross when he woke because he liked to be in charge of that sort of thing, reading the map, giving instructions. And all the time while he'd been asleep she had loved it, just driving along the road and deciding which way to go as the signposts came up and choosing one way or another on the spur of the moment. She'd seen a sign that had in brackets under it ('Secret Lake') written up like that, like the title of a poem or a story, with speech marks around it as though it were someone's private, special name for a place, and it had a little picture beside it, a silhouette of a little figure and there in smaller writing underneath were the words 'Memorial to Robert Burns ¾ mile' and an arrow. And she'd followed that.

They'd studied him in school of course, and Karl would have known a few of the poems by heart, no doubt, would have liked them too. But he hadn't been keen on the walk from the beginning. Waking like that to suddenly find himself somewhere that hadn't been planned for, wasn't in their itinerary, and yet there they were drawing up beside a picnic table and big municipal rubbish bin in a little car park dug out of the side of the road, with a board set up that gave walking directions to the lake and times it would take and the drawing of Robbie Burns and information all about him, and why he was Scotland's 'Most Loved Poet'.

Karl had stayed bad tempered while they pulled on their boots and jackets – jackets even though the winters were so mild there it was like summer at home, and people kept talking about the cold and sudden changes of weather but all Elisabeth could see was bright pacific blue sky all around her and the kind of sun that would make you brown if you lay in it and put suncream on. Not a winter at all. Even so, she did what he said, put her jacket on and they got ready in their usual way – and three quarters of a

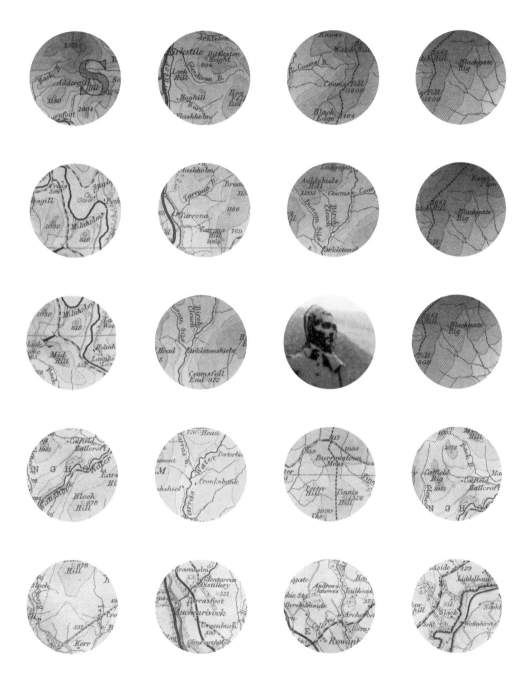

mile was nothing, she'd joked to Karl to cheer him up, they'd be in and out before he would notice they'd been gone.

They locked the car and headed into the opening in the bush that marked the beginning of a track. The bright day closed instantly behind them like a door. They were used to it by then, of course, from all their walks, the darkness, the close growth of the vegetation in this country that blocked out all the light. It had its own smell, its own particular damp and musky odour. You needed the tracks to be well marked or you'd be lost in a second, the low ferns and trees pushing in at you as you went deeper in and the high *totaras*, they were called, those amazing old and massive trees that grew not like trees growing in the woods at home exactly, but seeming to rise up out of all that other bush that was banked up around them … Made Elisabeth think of that line from another poet, nothing like Robbie Burns … 'Darkness visible'. Because that was what it was like there, looking into the dark, seeing the dark as your eyes adjusted, but as they walked on she didn't mind it either, Karl's back up ahead of her as the path inclined a little as though rising to a hill then flattening again. Certainly it had been an easy enough walk. The description on the board in the car park had not exaggerated the time it would take and after about twenty minutes she'd seen slices of bright water through clearings in the bush, the glinting reflections of the sun and then they'd stopped, Karl had, and she came up behind and he'd said 'There it is' and there it was: 'The Secret Lake'.

Later, years later, once Elisabeth had started reading again and knew where 'darkness visible' came, in Book Two of 'Paradise Lost' and why she'd always loved Milton … she'd found an essay by Rebecca West where she wrote about this lake. That had been like a secret, too, discovering that someone else knew about that place and had written about it … And she recognised the feeling that was described in the writing, of the surprise of seeing those sudden flashes of bright blue amongst the dark bush and then stopping and suddenly there it all was, this large and flat expanse of lakewater lying in the centre of the country, at its secret heart, wrapped around by *punga* and *totara* and *manuka*, all those trees and bushes she'd known the name of while she'd been there …
A clear wide open lake of blue in a place that anywhere else in the world would have picnickers gathering on its little beaches, boats pushed off on the water's surface or waterskiers criss-crossing one side to the other … But here was completely hidden from view.

They saw the Memorial statue immediately – down one end of the lake and set like a jewel on a green lawn that had been created for it specially. They walked up towards it, skirting the water when the path took them down to the sand and then turning back into the bush for the final corner where they came out to stand on the grass. It seemed both bigger and smaller when they got there – the poet standing legs apart, hands on hips and his head upturned as though to catch the sun, high enough that you couldn't make out an expression on the face but low enough that the whole thing was of a scale that felt lifelike and real … Weirdly present, somehow, the figure of the famous Scottish figure set down here in this faraway country, polished and shining, with his own green lawn about him even with the dark growth ever closer at his back and the hidden lost water coming lapping over the sand towards the base of his pedestal where the dates of his birth and his death were marked, and those words again, after a few lines of his verse, 'Scotland's Most Loved Poet'.

Immediately she'd wanted to take off her jacket and stay.
It was warm, now they were out here in this clearing in the sun, the statue threw a clean dark shadow on the bright grass and Elisabeth had lain down alongside it, stripping off her top and trousers, the feel of the bright sun on her head and face and body, like a pulse, a beat, the centre of the day above her and before her only blue … It did feel like summer, no matter what anyone in that country said, no matter what Karl said as he'd stayed standing there above her, alongside Robbie Burns, refusing to lie down, to sit even … So she'd just stretched out, hadn't she, the shadow of the poet beside her like a companion, her body long and lean and full of sun lying there on the grass.

She'd wanted to stay for the whole afternoon. She'd wanted to lie in the warmth and hear the lap, lap, lap of the blue water against the little beach, listen to the silence all around and the little sounds of birds she'd never heard before collecting in the tall trees. She'd wanted to stay all through the rest of the morning,

into the afternoon, all through the day, let the sun come down and still she would stay there … Not think about the next place they had to go to, or the next map to see … Not answer questions or make decisions, just keep herself whole in this state of absolute arrival she felt herself to be in now, like she'd felt in the car before with Karl asleep and she'd taken any turn she wanted, seen the sign and just followed it with her eyes. So it was like Karl may as well be asleep now. And she realised the little hard feeling in her stomach from before was gone, that little bit of undigestible nut, like metal or bone, was gone and everything felt light and easy and warm.

That feeling, she knows now, looking back on all this, of getting 'lost' on that holiday as Karl had said they were when he'd woken up to find himself somewhere unexpected, was not being lost at all. It was the feeling, at the minute of letting it fall over her and claim her as she lay on the grass, of herself, who she was, what she wanted, what she didn't want. That she didn't want to be pulled to her feet as Karl pulled her. Didn't want to go back into the bush and leave it all behind her, the bright open secret of the lake with its strange statue that had been like some kind of a marker, to make her feel that all was tended, the grass cut around it and the ironwork polished and cleaned so it glinted in the sun … That she knew where she was.

Still she had let herself be taken, her jacket draped back around her bare form, her trousers put into her arms. She'd looked at the brand new ring on her finger and she'd started getting dressed, Karl calling ahead of her, 'Come on! Come on! This whole crazy thing has been a complete waste of time!'

But the recognition of what that day had meant did come at last, and in full, thirteen years later with the second statue and on a wintry hill in Scotland, the only 'proper place' Karl had said, on that last walk they ever took together, 'for a statue of Robbie Burns to be'. And there he was, she thinks now, and she's pretty sure it was the same statue, remember? It's how this story began. Only the second one was not cared for and polished like the other in that other secret place, but with lichen smattering its tired body and on the base of the stand the words not clear, nor the numbers for the dates as they'd been worn away by weather, all those details gone. A sort of fence had been put up around it. Why? To stop people getting too close? To stop them harming the statue in some way? Who knows, but whatever the reason there was to be no lying down here in its shadow. No peace of silence, of bush and then the water and then the green.

And that's when she said to Karl, like she should have said to him that day long ago by the water, 'No.' He was still talking. Talking as he stood. As though she'd never said a word. Talking like he'd talked all the way on the walk across the cold hills, still making his confession, but saying over and over they would make a 'go of it anyhow' – wouldn't they? Old friends that they were, such great old friends. That they had that to remember, no matter what. All the interests they had, the hobbies they shared. It's what they had to hold onto, what they had to keep …

But then she said it again, like she should have said it before. 'No'. Finally saying it so he would hear. No point in remembering. No point in going on. And no, as well, to hold onto. And no, to keep. No, no, no, no, no and again no. Like the books in the bookshelf between the two bookends that stood like little statues either side, might all have pages inside them all filled with the single word. No. She'd twirled her ring, dropped it on the grass. And Karl was down on his hands and knees to hunt for the speck of stone in the heather while she was walking away.

Kirsty Gunn is Professor of Creative Writing at the University of Dundee. She was born in 1960 in New Zealand and is the award winning author of four novels, including Rain (Faber), for which she won a London Arts Board Literature Award and The Boy and the Sea (Faber), winner of the 2007 Sundial Scottish Arts Council Book of the Year Award.

THE SECRET

Robert Burns

From 'Tam O'Shanter: A Tale'

    Now, wha this tale o' truth shall read,
Ilk man and mother's son, take heed:
Whene'er to drink you are inclin'd,
Or cutty-sarks run in your mind,
Think, ye may buy the joys o'er dear:
Remember Tam o' Shanter's mare.

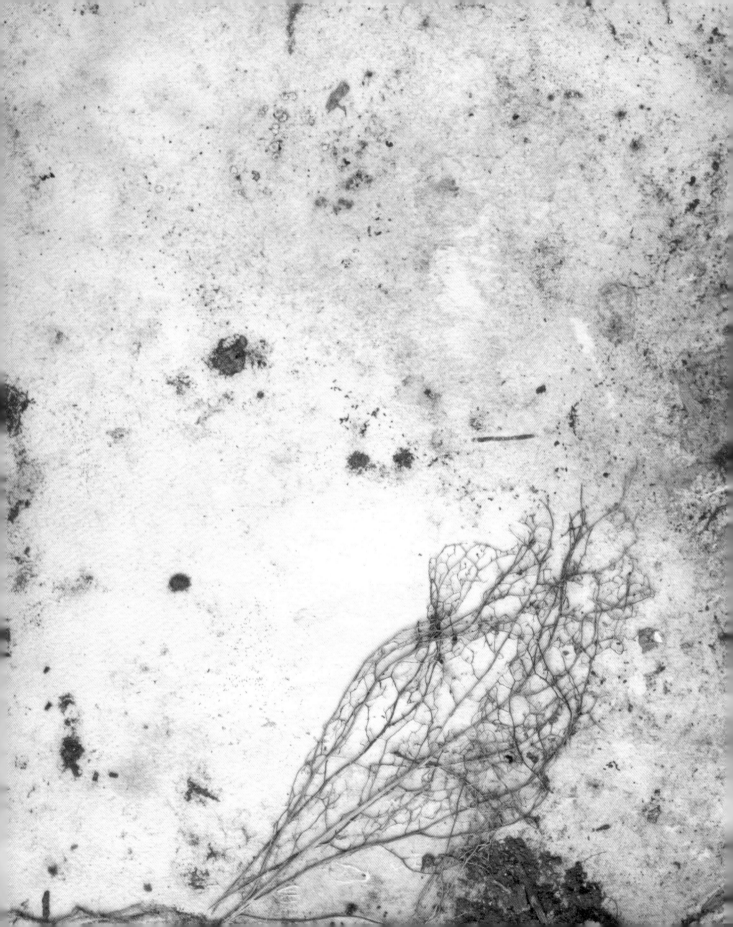

James Crossley

Red Rose

The farmer lent against the Aga for warmth. She was asleep in the rocking chair, lamb in her arms and empty colostrum bag on the floor. Looks like she's saved another one, he thought. He stood and looked at her, and smiled to himself when he saw the ends of her hair were still red. Had it been so long? But then, no, it hadn't really been very long ago at all. But the shop was gone.

The shop was at the far end of the town, fifty yards short of the Burns memorial. It was farther than he needed to go, but he went anyway. Drove that bit longer, and he hated to drive. Ten minutes there, ten back, and no lights anywhere, just black fields rolling away into the night. But then he'd driven in one late night, sugar for tea, and there she was. Her hair was black but she'd dyed it blood red, and she was young and pale and tried to talk small, but he kept his eyes low, murmured and was gone.

But he found he had taken her along with him, and at first he did not know why. She sat quietly in his mind and watched while he daily carried buckets of feed, and cleaned out the cattle courts, and baled the hay, and rebuilt the walls knocked over by leaning cattle and scampering sheep. And then the image began to fade because so long had passed since he had seen her, and so once more he drove into town.

She was sweeping the floor, red hair tied back. He picked up a tin of biscuits and took them to the counter and smiled and paid, and was gone, but once more with the memory of her.

But it was no longer enough, he wanted to know more of her. The farmer asked her questions in his mind; and then, when he could stand the frustration no longer, he climbed into his car and drove out to the shop just short of the memorial. Each time he intended to talk to her, to ask her questions, but he never did. He could not even ask her name.

Months past and he did not go to the shop. Then his father grew ill and died, and the farm was left to the farmer and his brother. His brother disappeared after the funeral and the farmer did not look for him. Perhaps if there had not been so much to do on the farm, but there was so much. The farmer fed the cattle and brought in the crops and sat for hours on a wooden chair in the doorway of the rumbling dryer. The farm had become the farmer's life, he worked and slept and was too tired to think.

And then one day he found there were no jobs to be done on the farm. The seeds had been sown and the cattle and sheep grazed quietly in well-walled fields. The farmer laughed to himself, contented by a feeling of fatigue and achievement. A cup of tea, he thought and returned to the farm house. But when he opened the pantry there were no biscuits, and then he thought of the girl and once more climbed into his car and drove out to the shop just short of the memorial.

But she was not there. Hilda was behind the counter, big and strong and old, but not as old as the farmer.

'A was sorry to hear about your father,' she said, and settled back into her bulk.

'It was a time ago.'

'We haven't seen you in here since. Hard thing… and you looking after the farm?'

'With my brother.'

'Aye.'

And then she appeared from somewhere unseen, red-haired and pale and with full lips and green eyes. Her coat was buttoned and she wore blue woollen gloves and had a white woollen hat she held in her right hand.

'I'm going now, Hilda.'

'Okay, Rosie.'

'That isn't my name.'

'Rose, then.'

Hilda rolled her yes and looked at the farmer, and then he looked at Rose and she at him, and he saw her blush before he looked away.

'So, is Billy picking you up?'

'No. You know I finished with him last week. Why did you ask that? I'm walking home.'

'Not in this weather you're not, Robert here will take you. You don't mind, do you Robert, on your way anyway.'

The farmer coughed and swallowed.

Silence and darkness in the car. The farmer stared ahead and tightly gripped the wheel, and Rose sat next to him, a tin of shortbread biscuits on her lap. Eventually Rose spoke.

'I love these biscuits.'

The farmer said nothing, did not even glance across at her.

'I love them in the winter with tea and when it's cold outside and there's snow on the ground.'

'Do you like them?' she asked.

And then suddenly, and all at once, the tightness in the farmer's shoulders and arms fell away and he turned to look at Rose.

'I like them very much,' he said.

Rose yawned and lifted an arm to stifle, and then her eyes opened.

'Hello,' she said, her head still lent back against the chair, the lamb sleeping quietly in her lap. 'Is everything all right down there?'

'Sure.'

'What is it, you've got a look, what are you thinking of?'

The farmer settled back in his chair, smiled a little, gripped the hot cup in his hand, and said: 'A shop. A Poet. A sheep. A girl. A boy.'

James Crossley has received a degree in English Literature, a degree in History, and a postgraduate degree in Writing Culture from the University of Dundee. He lives and works on a farm.

A SHOP

A POET

A SHEEP

A GIRL

A BOY

MY LOVE IS LIKE "BARD"
Words by Robert Burns

heart...

— Robert Burns
"Barn-yar-ball"

t not now, to draw hie frailties

Robert Burns

From 'To A Mouse'

But Mousie, thou art no thy-lane,
In proving *foresight* may be vain:
The best laid schemes o' *Mice* an' *Men*,
                 Gang aft agley,
An' lea'e us nought but grief an' pain,
                  For promis'd joy!

Still, thou art blest, compar'd wi' *me*!
The *present* only toucheth thee:
But Och! I *backward* cast my e'e,
                 On prospects drear!
An' *forward*, tho' I canna *see*,
                 I *guess* an' *fear*!

Jim Stewart

Meg

'Remember Tam o' Shanter's mare',
fur therebi hings a tale.
'A better never lifted leg'.
Fat lot o guid it did puir Meg,
whose bum wiz left full bare.

The trouble wi bein Tammy's horse
an skelpin thro the dubs,
is that yer rider's maistly pished
and drives ye thro the rain and mist
miles aff the proper course.

He taks ye past yon kirk at night
tae ogle naked witches.
Aw very weel fur him tae stop
an watch thae warlocks rave an bop
wi aw their unco sight;

but a horse like me hiz feelins tae,
an wanted oot the weather.
While he stauns gowpin wi bulgin een
at some hauf-strippit disco quean,
Ah'm thinkin o dry strae.

An then they bawlt some heathen curse
an wur headin at full tilt
to gain the keystane o the brig
as if this wiz a game o tig
when whit's at stake's mah arse,

which got its pride an joy ripped oot
bi yon bitch wi the sark,
an he lowps free abuin mah back
as the thunders an the lightnings crack,
an Ah'm fell pit aboot.

So noo Ah hudny goat yon tail
Ah used tae swish the flees,
while aff he flang scot-free fur hame
tae spill tae his sulky sullen dame
hoo much he'd spent on ale.

But there's a God. Fur Kate wiz waitin,
aw tappin foot an rollin pin.
As she bashed the maister's hauf-cut heid
(a bollockin tae mak ye bleed,
an mair, nae hesitatin)

Ah sank mah hurdies in the strae,
gratefu fur the barn's warmth,
listenin as each pummel landed
an screechin furious Kate demanded
reasons Tammy didna hae.

Ah fell asleep tae yon sweet rail,
an had nostalgick dreams
o meadows, flooers, rinnin streams
wioot sic ugsome dree
or ony hellicat besoms; an me
united wi mah tail.

Jim Stewart

Burns

Only heaven knew how he was taught,
how it was he found his chosen furrow;
and no man who puts hand to plough and looks
back is fit for the kingdom of God, it's said.
Brother to most men, he mocked some others;
loved women; fathered bairns; and pleased the great.
Behind a heavy horse, his keen blade caught
unopened ground and broke it for the harrow
of raking satire, as he shooed the rooks
black and cawing loud about his head.
Weight of work and failure, and of lovers,
the dirt and deity of human fate
embraced, he would observe religious lice;
and carved his field of lines, avoiding mice.

*Jim Stewart is a poet whose work has appeared in New
Writing Scotland, The Red Wheelbarrow, riverrun and
many other places. From time to time Jim reviews for
the Times Literary Supplement and has taught in the
University of Dundee's English Department since
the late 1980s.*

THE FARMER

Robert Burns

From 'The Cottars Saturday Night'

O SCOTIA! my dear, my native soil!
  For whom my warmest wish to Heaven is sent!
Long may thy hardy sons of *rustic toil*
  Be blest with health and peace and sweet content!
And O may Heaven their simple lives prevent
  From *Luxury*'s contagion, weak and vile!
Then howe'er *crowns* and *coronets* be rent,
  A *virtuous Populace* may rise the while,
And stand a wall of fire, around their much-lov'd ISLE.

O THOU! who pour'd the *patriotic tide*,
  That stream'd thro' great, unhappy WALLACE' heart;
Who dar'd to, nobly, stem tyrannic pride,
  Or *nobly die*, the second glorious part:
(The Patriot's GOD, peculiarly thou art,
  His *friend*, *inspirer*, *guardian*, and *reward*!)
O never, never SCOTIA's realm desert,
  But still the *Patriot*, and the *Patriot-bard*
In bright succession raise, her *Ornament* and *Guard*!

Standhall

Meikle Craigs

Lady Isle

MAP OF THE
LAND OF BURNS

BURNS

NAL

2

David Robb

Burns and the Longer View

On the A90 dual carriageway, about half a dozen miles south of Stonehaven, on the northbound carriageway near the mysteriously named Temple of Fiddes, there is a lay-by dominated by a rather imposing monument. The drivers who flash past it possibly assume, if they think about it at all, that it commemorates some ancient battle otherwise lost in the cobwebs of time. In actual fact, however, its purpose is a good deal more surprising. It reads:

This Memorial Cairn overlooks CLOCHNAHILL from which, between 1740-50, William Burnes the Father of Scotland's National Poet, left for EDINBURGH, and then AYRSHIRE. Erected by Wm. Coull ANDERSON, Esq. Florida, U.S.A., – a family descendant – 1968.

Every biography of Burns mentions that his family came from the North-East originally, but little is usually made of the point. It might be worth a moment's reflection here, however, for this memorial in particular reminds us of something not often brought to mind, namely that Burns's life and times – his moment in history – were part of the succession of generations in a family and in a society.

It would be entirely forgiveable to think of Burns as, essentially, the poet of the vivid moment. Does it not seem that his best – or at least his best-known – poems arise from, or evoke, tiny little episodes of human behaviour or experience? He is the poet of the one-off, of the unique moment. It is the sudden unexpected occurrences in life which appear to feed his imagination. He disturbs a mouse while he ploughs – and writes a poem about it. He ploughs up a mountain daisy – and writes a less effective poem about that. He spots a louse on a lassie's bonnet in church and writes a fine poem about that. One-off moments. When the auld farmer salutes his auld mare, he does so on New Year morning, specifically. The whole world of an impoverished, down-trodden Scottish cottar is conjured up and interpreted in a famous and controversial poem, but that world is created by an account of his Saturday night, solely.

Talking about single, specific nights ...

> Ae market-night,
> *Tam* had got planted unco right ...

'Ae market-night ...' – 'one market night': Burns's most famous poem is the story of a single night's adventure, as one-off as they come. Burns, however, can be even more specific in indicating when his tales (shaggy dog stories as they may sometimes be) allegedly occurred:

> ... Upon a bonie day in June,
> When wearing thro' the afternoon,
> *Twa dogs,* that were na thrang at hame,
> Forgather'd ance upon a time.

Other equally unlikely encounters take place in Burns's pages, but there is always at least a gesture towards precision of time – or as much precision as a drunken recollection will allow – and if certainty of time cannot be guaranteed then at least the specific location of the one-off adventure can be laboriously insisted upon:

> I was come round about the hill,
> And todlin down on *Willie's mill*,
> Setting my staff wi' a' my skill,
>   To keep me sicker;
> Tho' leewards whyles, against my will,
>   I took a bicker.

A noble attempt, that, at narrative precision despite the difficulties of befuddled recollection. And there are other nights in the pub, too, with time and place both specific and unique:

> ... Ae night at e'en a merry core
>   O' randie, gangrel bodies
> In Poosie-Nansie's held the splore,
>   To drink their orra dudies ...

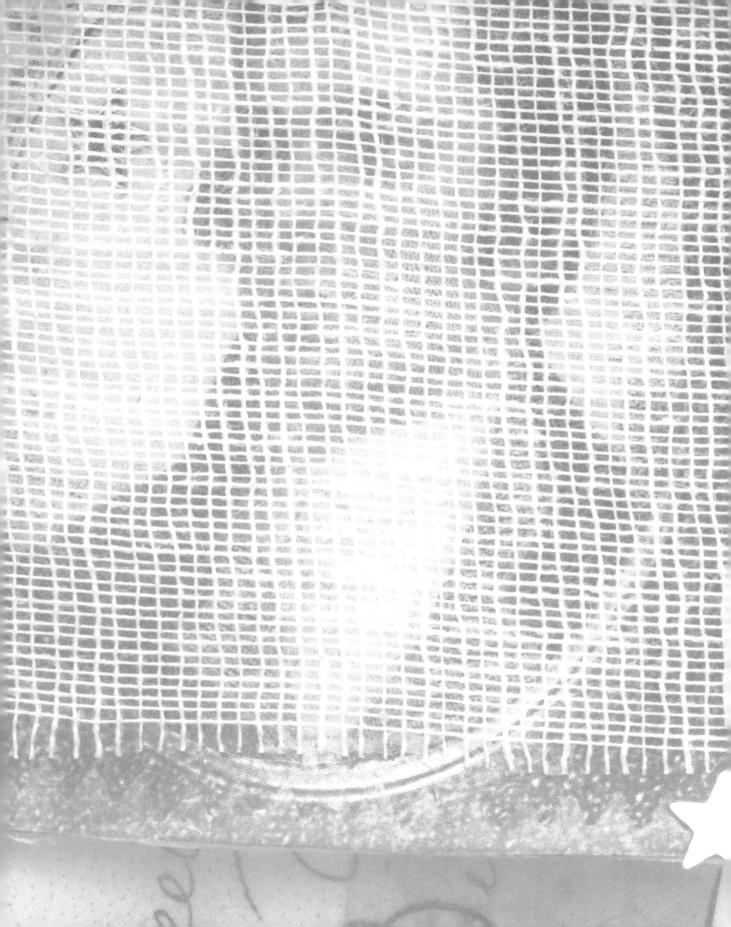

Nor is it merely this world's sinners who are pinned down, in their fallibility, to specific episodes of back-sliding; so are his saints. Holy Willie is imagined, for a few choice minutes only, sending up his twisted, self-justifying prayer to the Almighty. On yet another day, Burns takes us with him (and with that harum-scarum lassie, Fun) to laugh at the contradictions of a strange day-long get-together, the Holy Fair. Indeed, all his so-called Kirk Satires ('The Ordination', 'The Calf', 'The Kirk's Alarm', 'The Twa Herds', etc) are poems of the moment, partly in the sense that they reflect immediate local issues and personalities, but partly too in the sense that the vivid speaking voices which are their medium sound in our ears like people immediately beside us, praying, exclaiming, gasping, or laughing with life-like spontaneity. Indeed, the sense of Burns as the Poet of the Present Moment derives in no small part from that supple, dramatic Scots utterance in which his best poems are written.

Yet there is more to explain Burns's immediacy than just the sound of his voices – important as that is: Burns's appeal arises, in no small measure, from the accuracy of his brief and specific glimpses of real human experience – hence that feeling which Scottish people (especially) have had, from that time to this, \that Burns is the poet who speaks for us, and expresses what life actually feels like to live. We feel that Burns is living, from moment to moment, a life like ours. His verse epistles are the fine poems they are, in large measure, because we can sense the spontaneity and uniqueness of utterance which is the essential condition of any letter from one friend to another. Even his songs work, at their frequent best, by suggesting to us the thoughts and feelings of the moment – what is a love-song, in fact, but the apparent momentary overflow of powerful feeling? It is especially true of those songs in which Burns creates, in the speaker/singer of the song, a character distinct from

himself, like the desolate and defeated Jacobite bidding farewell to his beloved in 'It Was A' for Our Rightfu' King' or the ingeniously self-contradictory love-lorn lass besotted with Tam Glen.

Burns the poet of the present moment? Yes, that seems to cover a lot that is true about his poetry. What's more, a fixed, momentary memorability can also seem to be the hallmark of his life, just as it is of his verse. Doesn't Burns, in our minds, exist with special vividness in his own time and place, suddenly emerging out of the soil of Ayrshire in the later years of the eighteenth century to weave a story which takes on something of the fixedness and completeness of a legend (the youthful scrapes with the lasses, the great amours – Jean Armour, Highland Mary, Clarinda and the others, the brave little venture into provincial print which takes the world by storm and saves him from fleeing to the West Indies, the ploughman who, for a season, dominated Edinburgh's drawing-rooms, etc)? Does not our own sense of couthy kinship with 'Rabbie' serve to lift him out of Time into a timeless realm where every generation can encounter him afresh – and isn't that what Burns suppers are all about? He has become an icon – a fixed momentary image upon which we can load whatever meaning or significance we choose.

But the inscription on that unexpected memorial on the A90 provides us with a different perspective – on his life and maybe on his work, too. Robert Burns (1759-96) was the comparatively short-lived member of a family which stretched (like all families) through time and space. His immediate forebears knew a very different part of Scotland from the Ayrshire we associate with him, and he had relatives and descendants who travelled to distant parts of the world – Florida (in at least one case, as the inscription indicates), but also London (his son Robert); India

(two other sons, and his grand-daughter Eliza); Guelph, Ontario –
for a while, anyway (another grand-daughter, Jane Emma);
Australia (his grand-daughter Sarah); Vancouver (his great-great-
grandson Robert Burns Hutchison). And this is only the tip of
the iceberg – as is perhaps only to be expected when we are
considering a progenitor as vigorous and as little constrained by
matrimony as Robert Burns. The iconic poet, we should scarcely
need to remind ourselves, was as embedded in time as the rest
of us. That brief Ayrshire life was part of a much longer view.
The roadside memorial speaks doubly: it reminds us that Burns
had family before and after his own life, and it is itself a device
whereby a past is connected with a future – for as long as that
rather sturdy stone cairn stands. It enfolds Burns in the longer
view of the reality of time's passing.

Was that longer view, so important and unavoidable an aspect of
human experience, ignored by this great poet of the moment –
so greatly given to living in each instant as he was? No, he did
not ignore it – although his technique of creating so many vivid
episodes can rather obscure the fact. When we look again at
his poetry, it is not so hard to see longer perspectives being
acknowledged or reflected in it. The passing generations
have their place in it, also. The cottar may have relaxed, and
worshipped, on a very specific Saturday night – it was the night,
for one thing, that his beloved daughter Jenny first brought home
her Jo (and, can we doubt it, her future husband?). Yet this same
cottar stands in the poem for a whole class and, even more, for
the rugged honesty, humanity and piety which Burns sees as a
peculiar and (significantly) traditional and ancient strength of
generations of Scots.

> From scenes like these, old Scotia's grandeur springs …

Nor is his gaze solely on the past and present: contemplating his
cottar, he is looking to the future, too.

> Long may thy hardy sons of *rustic toil*
>   Be blest with health and peace and sweet content!
> And O may Heaven their simple lives prevent
>   From *Luxury*'s contagion, weak and vile!
> Then howe'er *crowns* and *coronets* be rent,
>   A *virtuous Populace* may rise the while,
> And stand a wall of fire, around their much-lov'd ISLE.

He has other patriotic backward glances: a sense of history and
of continuities can emerge anywhere in his thoughts, as when he
contemplates his own immediate district in 'The Vision'. Here,
for example, he praises the virtues of the inhabitants,
past and present, of the town of Ayr:

> Low, in a sandy valley spread,
> An ancient BOROUGH rear'd her head;
> Still, as in *Scottish Story* read,
>   She boasts a *Race*,
> To ev'ry nobler virtue bred,
>   And polish'd grace.

'Scots Wha Hae', it seems, is not the only nationalistic evocation
of the past in Burns's work.

> At WALLACE' name, what Scottish blood,
> But boils up in a spring-time flood!
> Oft have our fearless fathers strode
>   By WALLACE' side,
> Still pressing onward, red-wat-shod,
>   Or glorious dy'd!

Nor were full-blown patriotic feelings the only ones to prompt
him to consider his place in the larger scheme of passing time. He
had a profound sense of gratitude to his poetic predecessors:

> O for a spunk o' ALLAN's glee,
> Or FERGUSON's the bauld an' slee …

Robert Fergusson (1750-74) in particular was much in his
thoughts:

> O *Ferguson!* thy glorious *parts*
> Ill-suited *law*'s dry, musty arts!
> My curse upon your whunstane hearts,
>   Ye Enbrugh Gentry!
> The tythe o' what ye waste at *cartes*
>   Wad stow'd his pantry!

And he was prepared to put his money where his mouth was,
as Fergusson's gravestone, which Burns paid for, proclaims in
Edinburgh's Canongate kirkyard – the achievement of the past
projected into the future by Burns's generous largeness of vision.
Less physically solid, but even more crucial in preserving for the
future the cultural wealth of the past was his selfless endeavour in
preparing for publication the texts of all the Scottish folksongs he
provided for Johnson's Scots Musical Museum and then for
Thomson's 'Select Collection of Original Scottish Airs'.
Furthermore, we can say that where his poetry is built on the
traditions which came down to him from earlier times – whether
the tradition was that of folksong and folktale, or whether it was
the methods and techniques of poets like Ramsay and Fergusson
– his work becomes something of a tradition-bearer itself.

He has at least one poem – one of his unlikely tall tales – which deals directly with these matters (the changefulness of things over time). This is his 'The Brigs of Ayr', in which he fancifully claims to overhear an argument between the spirits of the two bridges – one an ancient structure and the other a modern affair – as to their respective merits. The poem becomes a debate between the virtues of the contemporary in general, as against the value, claims and durability of the ancient and traditional. Burns does not seem to make a final choice between them, but the poem shows him to be fully alive to the passing of ages, and to the living rhythms which exist in time. The seasons pass, and so do the generations of living creatures – creatures who are all eventually cruelly cut down, one way or another, like the birds wantonly slain each autumn by sportsmen, as the poem describes.

> The thund'ring guns are heard on ev'ry side,
> The wounded coveys, reeling, scatter wide;
> The feather'd field-mates, bound by Nature's tie,
> Sires, mothers, children, in one carnage lie.

Most directly of all, his concern for 'sires, mothers, children' surfaces in various ways throughout his verse, revealing his immediate sense of the passing generations. He can proffer 'A Poet's Welcome to His Love-Begotten Daughter'; he can glorify the splendid spirit of the lass made pregnant by 'Rob … the rantin' dog the daddie o't'; he can transform an excellent anonymous song of married sexuality into 'John Anderson My Jo', that equally excellent song celebrating the worth and satisfaction of a long, loyal married life; he can praise and acknowledge his own father both directly and indirectly – directly in the portrait of 'the priest-like Father' of 'The Cottar's Saturday Night', and indirectly in 'Tam o' Shanter', that most imaginative and entertaining comic memorial he built in words over his father's grave in the churchyard of Kirk Alloway.

No, Burns was sufficiently alive to the longer view of human life, even though we may paradoxically feel that it is when he evokes the vivid human moment (rather than when he moralises in empty generalities) that he communicates it most successfully.

Dr David Robb is a senior Lecturer at the University of Dundee. His latest book, Auld Campaigner: A Life of Alexander Scott (Dunedin Academic Press), was the joint winner of the Scottish Research Book of the Year, 2007 prize from the Saltire Society and National Library of Scotland and was shortlisted for the Sundial Scottish Arts Council book of the year awards in non-fiction.

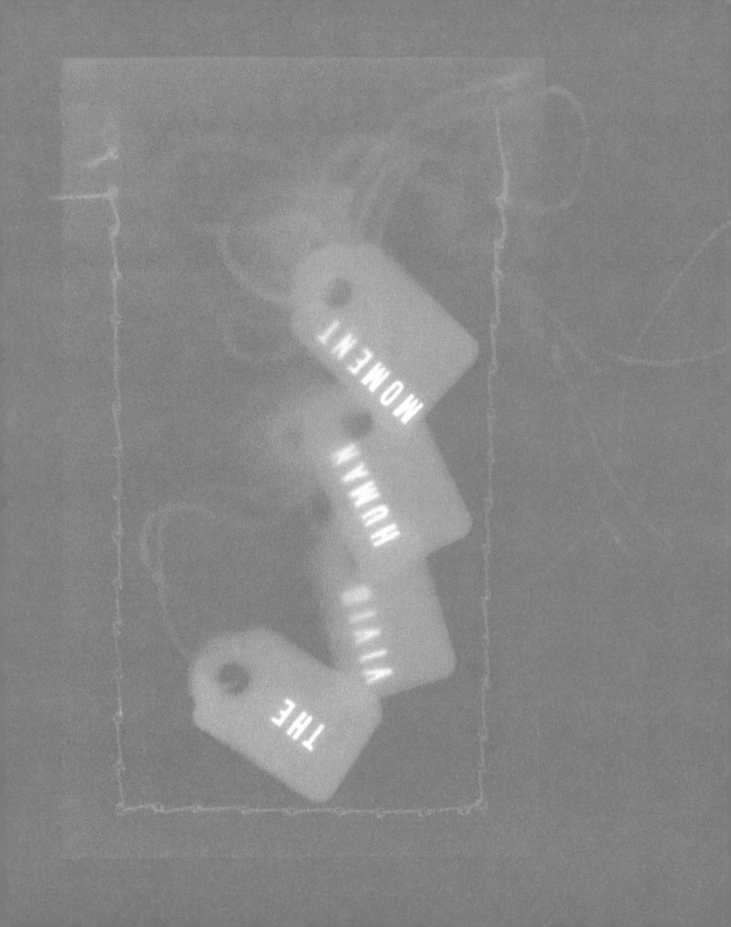

Robert Burns

Epistle to Davie

O, all ye *Pow'rs* who rule above!
O THOU whose very self art *love*!
  THOU know'st my words sincere!
The *lifeblood* streaming thro' my heart,
Or my more dear *Immortal part*,
  Is not more fondly dear!
When heart-corroding care and grief
  Deprive my soul of rest,
Her dear idea brings relief
  And solace to my breast.

She has my heart,
she has my hand,
By sacred truth and
honour's band.
Till the mortal stroke
shall lay me low,
I'm thine, my Highland
lassie, O.

— Robert Burns, from
"The Highland Lassie"

Stewart McCarthy

Ploughman's Naked Lunch

I sit at the foot of the statue. I stare up at him but He does not return my stare. He looks out. Looks through the city. I stare up at him. My eyes are wet.

It is windy and it is cold. He is cold-looking brass. The city is busy. I want to run away with him. He is too heavy to hold.

People would see. He would see.

It is grey here. If I wear a bright scarf He will see me and He will surely look. He will look if it is red. I buy a red scarf and jump up and down in front of him. He does not look.

I wait for the clouds to pass. They do pass because of the wind. He glints in the sun.

I climb up to where his foot rests. He is huge. His feet are bigger than mine. I lay my bag down on his plinth and eat my packed lunch.

I offer him a sandwich but he does not look or acknowledge me. I eat the sandwich myself.

It clouds over again. I read him one of his own poems. He does not react.

Maybe He doesn't remember.

I climb up onto his lap, his huge thighs, and strain to whisper in his ear. I tell him I have just read one of his poems. I tell him I love him.

I think he nods but I can't be sure.

It's getting dark.

I climb down from beside his ear and down onto the plinth and then onto the ground. I take off the red scarf. I take off my shirt and trousers and shoes and socks. I put on the red scarf again and climb back up onto his lap. The brass is cold against my legs. It is very cold now.

He seems to like me sitting there.

Nobody on the street looks up. I don't look down. He looks through the city.

I climb up onto his shoulders. I lean forward to give him a peck on the cheek.

Nobody looks.

Stewart McCarthy did his undergraduate degree at the University of Dundee and is currently completing his MA Creative Writing at the University of Manchester. He has previously had short stories published in 'New Writing Dundee' and 'Bewilderbliss'.

FOR A' THAT
AND A' THAT..."

Christopher A Whatley

Burns, the 'People's Poet', and Dundee?

Unlike Burns and Ayr, Burns and Dumfries, Burns and Edinburgh even, Burns and Dundee don't resonate in the way the other pairings do. Robert Burns' family hailed from the Mearns, the expanse of farmland that straddles Kincardineshire and north Angus, the county of which Dundee was the premier town – but that is stretching the connection. Burns, however, did once stop over in Dundee, during his tour of the Highlands in 1787. The city, then only a town, albeit one of Scotland's ancient royal burghs, he described as a pleasant, low-lying place. Other than that, silence.

But if Dundee left only a fleeting impression on Burns – albeit a more favourable one than others who visited the town towards the end of the eighteenth-century – Burns made a lasting mark on Dundee. The most visible sign of this is the squat-looking but imposing bronze statue of Burns that since 1880 has sat on a pedestal of Peterhead granite in Albert Square. Necessarily invisible however, is the determination there was amongst its proponents to have a statue of Burns erected in Dundee. Statues in Ayr, Dumfries, Edinburgh, Kilmarnock, Paisley and even Glasgow make more immediate sense, given Burns' associations with south-west Scotland and his initial reception amongst Edinburgh's literati, but Dundee? Explanation is needed.

Several memorials to Burns were erected in the first half-century following his death, notably the monuments in Dumfries (1818), Alloway (1820) and Edinburgh (1831). However the focus of public interest at this time was to know Burns better. Numerous editions of his works appeared, as did several biographies, whilst newspapers printed reminiscences of those who had been personally acquainted with Burns (and members of his family), and those who wished they'd been closer. There was a yearning too for physical contact, albeit at second hand. Alloway Kirk – of 'Tam o' Shanter' fame, and where Burns' father, William, was buried - was all but stripped bare of any of its surviving wood, by plundering visitors seeking fragments, as in former times they

would have purloined or purchased holy relics. In 1843 a visitor to Burns' cottage (then a public house), was struck by the tables and chairs that had been 'cut and hacked with thousands of names and initials', and the similarly-scratched windows. There was a macabre interest in Burns' bones, while phrenologists practised their quack-science by reading his skull but revealing nothing worth knowing. Burns' widow Jean Armour drew as big a crowd for her funeral as her late husband's had almost forty years earlier, while the mausoleum in St Michael's churchyard, Dumfries, where her remains were laid alongside those of Burns, became a shrine for reverential pilgrims: a Scottish Jerusalem for a secular saint.

Other relatives benefited from the patronage of the nation's great and good, with some contributions being made to assuage the guilt of those concerned at allowing Burns to die in distress: Scotland's eighteenth-century shame. On their return from lengthy service in India, Burns' sons found themselves fêted – and mobbed in the manner of the Beatles in their hey-day – by a massive surging crowd at a festival in Ayr in 1844, organised in their honour, and in memory of their father. The festival's organisers had other ends in mind however: to persuade the thousands of agricultural and other workers and listeners present that the stoical, patriarchal virtues extolled in Burns' 'Cottar's Saturday Night' should be theirs too, and that they should therefore endure their lot, and eschew the violence that was sweeping parts of the English countryside.

It was not until the final third of the nineteenth century that Scotland's towns began to vie with each other to declare in stone and bronze their association with Scotland's bard. Earlier in the century statues had been raised in some Scottish cities to commemorate more traditional 'great men' – but mainly (but not exclusively) establishment figures such as generals, politicians and inventors, and Sir Walter Scott.

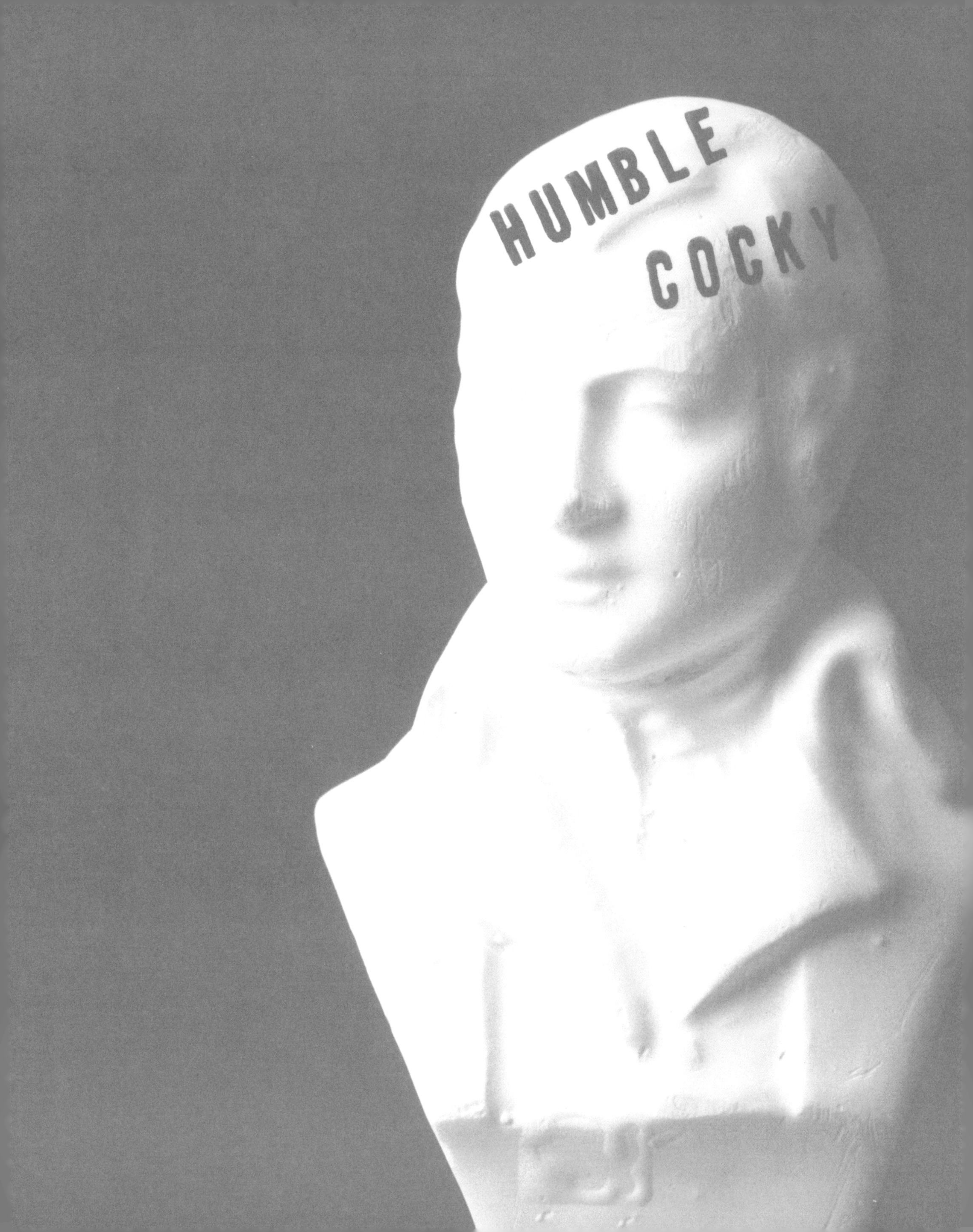
HUMBLE
COCKY

Albeit that the main push to erect permanent memorials to Burns began belatedly, in the wake of what for many was the unexpected nationwide efflorescence of centenary celebrations marking his birth in 1859, what is striking is the enthusiasm there was to commemorate and memorialise Burns. By no means was this confined to Scotland. Scots abroad devoured Burns' works. Nostalgia and longing induced many to contribute to memorial funds back home, but there were other impulses too, which culminated in statues of Burns across the Scottish Diaspora. Scotland's most sculpted son, Burns was and is a global phenomenon.

Of the post-1859 wave, Glasgow was first. Dundee went (almost) for broke, and employed the pre-eminent Scottish sculptor Sir John Steell, whose links with Dundee included previously commissioned public works, notably a full-size statue of the town's Radical MP, George Kinloch. Cannily, however, the statue committee was able to use the model Steell had designed for a Burns statue to be erected in New York's Central Park, so what Dundee got was a smaller, lower-cost version. But it was judged by many to be a fine statue nevertheless, its admirers being struck by the poet's romantic pose, and the realism of Steell's figure of Burns.

As in most places, the initial impetus for the statue came from prominent citizens who were also Burns enthusiasts. In the Rev George Gilfillan, Dundee could boast one of the country's most ardent Burnsians. A campaigning, anti-aristocratic, democratically-inclined, hypocrisy-hating United Presbyterian divine, Gilfillan published several editions and studies of Burns' work, and spoke eloquently on his behalf. And in his defence, preaching the case for Christian forgiveness against those moralising mid-Victorian kirk-men who condemned Burns-worship as a stain on Scotland's soul. Also active was A C Lamb, proprietor of a temperance hotel in Reform St, and an avid antiquarian who amassed a major collection of Burns' works and ephemera. But amongst ordinary people too, there was support for the efforts of the organising committee of councillors, lawyers, employers and other local leaders. Indeed Dundee's Burns Club, founded in 1860, was marked by 'the atmosphere of a working men's club', a factor, apparently, that led to the formation of the more genteel Dundee Burns Society, in 1896. But from 1878 if not earlier, the Burns Club put its weight behind the campaign for a statue.

It was the unveiling ceremony however, that revealed just what Burns meant to Dundee's inhabitants. Assembled in Albert Square itself, were between 25,000 and 40,000 people. This was equivalent to as much as one-third of the town's population. Another half lined the gaily decorated streets or hung from windows or stood on roof tops to watch the spectacular procession of 7,000 or 8,000 which included not only civic dignitaries but also, and mainly, the massed ranks of Dundee's trades and societies. Accompanied by several music bands – most of which comprised army volunteers – they proudly displayed their trade emblems and flags, as well carrying with them the tools of their trades, and sometimes even, examples of the products they made. Their banners announced common themes that resonated with their understanding of what Burns stood for: independence, the dignity of man, friendship, mutual support and unity.

This public, popular display of ardour for Burns should occasion no surprise. Much earlier – even at the time of his funeral, in Dumfries on 25 May 1796 – it was clear that Burns was perceived to have been an extraordinary Scot, even if in the last years of his life he had been spurned by the establishment in Scottish society that had hailed him in Edinburgh as the 'heaven-taught' ploughman. In this guise he was safe, compared to the republican he would become, and, close to his deathbed, he was anxious to be remembered as – although not beyond the walls of home and his favoured hostelries. Regardless (and anyway Burns had latterly joined the loyalist volunteers as the threat of invasion from France loomed larger), Dumfries was besieged for the occasion of his funeral, indicative perhaps of the recognition that with Burns' death, something of the 'ancient and once [independent] Scottish nation' had died too.

This is important, as, locked into the political union of 1707 that had created the United Kingdom of Great Britain, it was largely through its oral and written culture that Scotland survived – and has in the twentieth and now the twenty-first century flourished, devolution notwithstanding. But getting to this point has been difficult. Elements of Scotland's identity – including the country's history, language and literature – had been under threat for centuries; since the Reformation in the case of written Scots. The eroding process of Anglicisation and the centralising tendencies of London continued through the eighteenth and nineteenth centuries. It was against these subtle but powerful

Before the proudest of the earth

We stand with an uplifted brow;

Like us THOU wast a toil-worn man,

And we are noble now!

forces – although not union itself – that Sir Walter Scott railed in his *Letters of Malachi Malagrowther* (1826). Recognising that the Scots' language and dialect were the genetic markers of Scottish-ness, without which, according to Henry Cockburn, we 'lose *ourselves*', Burns was marshalled by patriotic Scots in the nineteenth century in the cause of cultural resistance.

In this regard Burns' appeal was broad and deep; in the words of the leading late Victorian Liberal, Lord Rosebery, Scotland's 'uncrowned king' from the 1880s, it was Burns who, at a time when Scotland was losing respect and identity, seemed 'to start to his feet and reassert Scotland's claim to national existence; his notes rang through the world, and he preserved the Scottish language forever.' In Dundee, Gilfillan was of the same mind, although like many nineteenth-century Scots for whom Burns was the carrier of Scottish culture, he saw no contradiction between the assertion of Scotland's distinctiveness, the demand for national dignity, and support for the United Kingdom of Great Britain and the global British Empire – a position that falls within the compass of what has been called 'unionist-nationalism', or even 'banal unionism'. In Dundee, with its dependence upon India for the raw material of its staple industry, jute, and empire markets for at least part of its sale, it could hardly be otherwise. Little wonder then that for the October 1880 unveiling of the Burns statue, the Harbour and Cowgate Porters carried aloft a banner printed with the words, 'Rule Britannia for the interest of thy people'.

But this shouldn't detract from the fact that it was in the role of collector and adapter of older Scottish song that Burns was paramount. Janice Galloway in this volume recalls her awareness of Burns' songs prior to her appreciation of them. This is precisely how countless Scots stretching back to Burns' own lifetime and certainly shortly afterwards, first encountered, and loved, Burns. Song, declared the Aberdeen Journal in 1859, was the 'old art of Scotland', but it was also an art form that was accessible to virtually everyone, simply by being sung, or printed in cheap and therefore affordable broadsheets and chapbooks. Song was the sound of everyday life, in the home, on the fields and in the workshop, and for many, an alternative to the sermon. Song lifted spirits. Burns' song had particular resonance for working people, evoking the natural world at a time of rampant urban growth and mechanisation, but also in the sense that by instilling a sense of human self-worth regardless of background or class, several of his

songs were lyrical manifestos not only for their own time but which also transcend time.

Easily overlooked in the more or less democratic, meritocracy in which we live today, is how radical many of Burns' poems and songs were for his largely vote-less contemporaries and their successors. For Burns' early audiences prior to the Reform Acts of 1832 and 1868, lowly social rank and meagre incomes equated with demeaning social status. Ostensibly, and often in reality, landlords in the countryside and employers in the towns held the whip hand. Portrayed as the ploughman poet, and therefore a man of modest rank himself, Burns – early on in the nineteenth-century accorded the title 'people's poet' – inspired generations of worker-poet-imitators, not a few of whom were either from or lived and worked in Dundee. If much – but by no means all – of their poetry is laboured in style and mawkish in tone, and falls short of the standards set by modern day literary critics, it was also heart-felt and based on real-life experience.

Just how influential Burns was in this respect can be seen by looking at William Nicoll, the son of a small tenant farmer and farm labourer near Perth. Described by Ebeneezer Elliot as 'Scotland's second Burns', Nicoll arrived in Dundee in 1836, and opened a short-lived circulating library. Politically a Radical, and acquainted with Dundee's Chartists, Nicoll acknowledged his debt to Burns not only in his choice of subject matter, but also in his *Poems and Lyrics*, in which he sub-titled the third section, following Burns' Kilmarnock edition, 'Poems Chiefly in the Scottish Dialect, Illustrative of the Feelings of the Intelligent and Religious Among the Working Classes in Scotland'. The first of these was entitled 'Stanzas on the Birthday of Burns'. The fourth of the stanzas announces – or at least anticipates – a social revolution:

> Before the proudest of the earth
> We stand with an uplifted brow;
> Like us THOU wast a toil-worn man,
> And we are noble now!

Although Nicoll's time in Dundee was brief, and his life tragically short, his legacy in part was Dundee's 'Republic of Letters'. This was an informal gathering of literate, politically-active working people, which encouraged the practice, later enhanced by Gilfillan's patronage, of working-class writing,

often with a radical, socially-levelling edge. Dundee too was one of a number of Scottish towns with a 'Poet's Box', an institution which offered impecunious writers the opportunity to publish their work – and to read that of others - in broadsheet form at the cost of a penny or less.

Unhappily for the cultural reputation of Dundee, with whom he has been irrevocably linked, it was this hotbed of aspirant literary genius that gave succour to William McGonagall. On the Saturday when the Burns statue was unveiled, Dundee's self-styled 'poet and tragedian' – decked in full Highland garb for the occasion – joined in the procession with the few surviving members of the Weavers Lodge of Lochee, of which he was a member. Expecting – apparently – to be invited to join the platform party, 'he proudly strutted along the whole route, as if conscious that the divine afflatus rested upon him as well as it did Robert Burns.' His hopes however were disappointed, and McGonagall cut a lonely and disconsolate figure, denied the opportunity of giving a rendition of his latest poem, in praise of Sir John Steell and the statue. Consequently McGonagall had little difficulty empathising with the rejection Burns experienced in his last years, and wrote, with feeling, in his 1897 'Ode to the Immortal Bard of Ayr, ROBERT BURNS', of the 'sorrows of the poor poet/When he's in want of *bread*'. The poem culminated in a personalised appeal for help 'while living', as 'he [the poet] requires no help when he's *dead*.'

Much earlier, but also influenced by Burns was William Thom, the Inverurie-born hand-loom weaver and part-time poet, who also spent time – and was to die – in Dundee. Tellingly, when recalling his indebtedness to the 'Song Spirits' that had had the effect of lifting the heart of the 'fagged weaver', Thom referred specifically to Burns' song, 'A man's a man for a' that'. In similar vein, a 'New Song on the Proposed Burns Statue in Dundee' which circulated on the streets of Dundee from around 1877, called on the working classes to 'agitate ower a' the toun' for the statue, on the grounds of Burns' humanity, his fame (as a Scot), and his capacity to light with 'smiles o' rarest joy the darkness o' despair', but above all because Burns had 'raised the head o' poverty, and lowed the might o' wrong.' It was sentiments of this kind that brought speakers on Burns their loudest ovations, as at the ceremony to unveil Dundee's Burns statue, when the Liberal MP Frank Henderson, declared to the approving crowd that the 'true secret' of Burns' popularity was that:

He shed a glory round the struggles of honest poverty. He lifted labour from the ditch and set it upon a throne.

> The honest man, tho' ne'er so poor,
> Is king o' men for a' that. (Cheers)

He showed that the nobility of the soul was confined to no rank in life … that peers were the creation of earthly kings, but that the honest man was the noblest work of God himself. (Cheers) … Under the inspiration of these two ideas with which Burns … furnished him – the essential dignity of his labour and the possible nobility of his life – the Scottish working man became transformed. (Cheers)

'Deafening and protracted' cheering followed Henderson's speech, prior to the unveiling itself. The Union Jack under which the statue was shrouded was hoisted away, while adding to the aural dimension of the proceedings, the Artillery Volunteers fired the first salute from the twelve guns placed nearby.

Not everyone was persuaded that Steell's statue or indeed most of the other Burns statues erected in Victorian Scotland prior to 1890 adequately reflected Henderson's reading of Burns. But it was Steell's statue that drew the sharpest criticism: a 'multiplied monstrosity' was how one hostile viewer put it. Burns, he went on, was 'not a model of grace', but 'there is no ground for believing that he was a hunchback.' Little wonder then that Steell made changes to the versions of his Dundee (and New York) Burns when requests for the same statue came from London and Dunedin. Forewarned by Scottish-American entrepreneur and Burns enthusiast Andrew Carnegie that he would be reluctant to fund any statue that resembled Steell's 'hump-backed simpleton', campaigners for a Burns statue in Montrose made sure that they found a different sculptor who would work to a very different design.

But the rage for statues and the passion for Burns grew less intense. Raising funds took longer. The proposal for a statue in Montrose was first mooted in 1882, but it was not unveiled until 1913. Arbroath's Burns statue took even longer to see the light of day, in 1959, seventy years after it was suggested. Why? Much of what Burns had stood for had been achieved. Increasingly – although this tendency had always been present – Burns was

plundered by politicians and claimed for party ends. The former consensus fragmented. And great men, so beloved by Victorians, were found to have feet of clay.

The shifting mood is reflected in Dundee where as early as 1889 the Burns statue was in need of repair. At the same time, in the town council, there was a proposal that the lettering should be filled in using white paint rather than gilt. The move was rejected, but even so it is indicative that Burns may have been held in less high regard in some quarters. Later Burns' name was carved into the pedestal. Was its omission an oversight in 1880? Or had Burns become less well-known, so much so that passers-by had to be told who the statue represented? While the Burns clubs (there were two in Dundee, one in Lochee) continued to meet, the Burns Society seems to have disappeared sometime following the Second World War. Wreaths continued to be laid at the foot of the Burns statue, but in January 1959, the 200th anniversary of Burns' birth, the ceremony was attended by a few hundred people rather than the thousands who had been present in 1880. Elsewhere in Scotland, Burns memorials – in Ayr, Kilmarnock and Mauchline to name but three – fell into disrepair, and in some cases were closed to intending visitors.

But Burns continues to attract attention, at home and abroad. Indeed in Scotland at large there has been a recent resurgence of interest in and enthusiasm for Burns. Certainly the Burns Supper season is as lively as ever, perhaps even more so. 'Scots Wha Hae' is promoted as a possible anthem for Scotland – as it was more than a century beforehand. There are a number of reasons for this revival. Above all there is the renewed confidence in Scottish culture, past, present and future, underpinned by the rise and establishment in power of the Scottish National Party. Burns' importance as a Scottish cultural icon has been recognised,

not least as his value to Scotland's economy has been estimated at around £160 million per annum. The potential of Burns to increase this by attracting tourists and even permanent settlers was seized by the Scottish Government in its Year of Homecoming campaign of 2009, at the centre of which is the fact of the 250th anniversary of Burns's birth. In this Scotland's national rulers are simply following a long-established tradition where Burns is concerned. In 1813 one of the leading advocates of the Burns mausoleum in Dumfries argued for its support on the grounds that the mausoleum would be an 'ornament' for the town, and bring 'strangers amongst us in their travels thro' Scotland.'

Most visitors from abroad or tourists from Scotland will nowadays be drawn to the Burns Heritage Park in Ayrshire, and the National Trust for Scotland's revamped (in 2010) Robert Burns Birthplace Museum. But there is a case too for venturing to Dundee and sensing, in the aura of Steell's statue, something of the 'heart-beatings' of Victorian Scotland, and the nation's adulation of the 'Immortal Bard of Ayr'.

Christopher A Whatley is Professor of Scottish History, and a Vice-Principal, University of Dundee. He wrote The Scots and the Union (Edinburgh University Press), and has long-standing interests in Robert Burns.

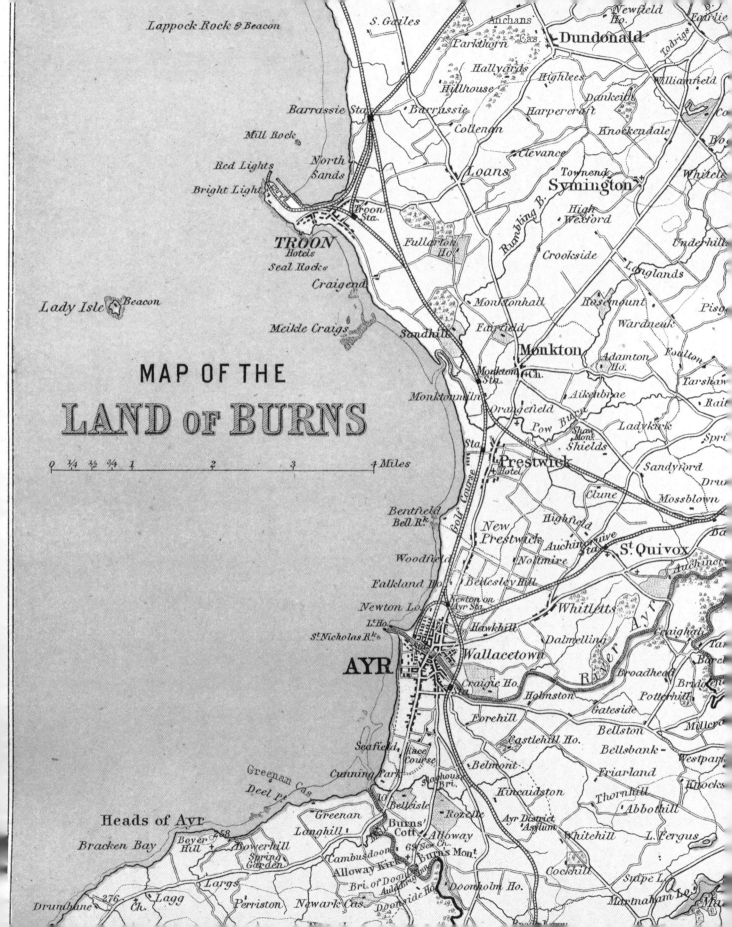

MAP OF THE
LAND of BURNS

0   ¼ ½ ¾ 1   2   3   4 Miles

Lappock Rock & Beacon

S. Gailes

Anchans

Newfield Ho.

Fairlie

Dundonald

Todrigs

Parkthorn

Hallyards

Highlees

Williamfield

Co

Barrassie Sta.

Barrassie

Hillhouse

Harpercroft

Dankeith

Ho.

Collenan

Knockendale

Clevance

Mill Rock

Loans

Townend

Whitele

Red Lights

North
Sands

Symington

High
Wexford

Bright Light

Troon
Sta.

Fullarton
Ho.

Rambling B.

Crookside

Underhill

Longlands

TROON

Hotels

Seal Rock

Craigend

Monktonhall

Rosemount

Pisg

Meikle Craigs

Sandhill

Fairfield

Wardneuk

Lady Isle   Beacon

Monkton

Adamton
Ho.

Foulton

Monkton
Sta.   Ch.

Aikenbrae

Tarshaw

Monktonmiln

Orangefield

Pow Burn

Shaw
Mont
Shields

Ladykirk

Rait

Sta.

Sandyford

Spri

Prestwick

Hotel

Clune

Dru

Bentfield
Bell R.

Golf Course

New
Prestwick

Highfield

Mossblown

Auchingrive

Woodfield

Notmire

Sta.

St. Quivox

Auchinc

Falkland Ho.

Bellesley Hill

Ba

Newton Lo.

Newton on
Ayr Sta.

Whitletts

Craighal

Lt. Ho.

Hawkhill

Dalmelling

Tar

St. Nicholas Rk.

Wallacetown

Holmston

Broadhead

Borel

AYR

Craigie Ho.

Sta.

Potterhill

Brid

Forehill

Gateside

Millcr

Seafield

Race
Course

Holmston

Bellston

Castlehill Ho.

Bellsbank

Cunning Park

Mosshous
Bri.

Belmont

Kincaidston

Friarland

Westpar

Greenan Cas.

Greenan

Burns'
Cott.

Bellisle

Rozelle

Ayr District
Asylum

Thornhill

Abbothill

Knocks

Heads of Ayr

Deel P.

Longhill

Alloway

Whitehill

L. Fergus

Bracken Bay

Boyer
Hill

Bowerhill

Spring
Garden

Cambusdoon

Alloway Kirk

Burns Mont.

Cockhill

Largs

Bri. of Doon

Doonholm Ho.

Snipe L.

Drumbane

Lagg

Ch.

Perriston

Newark Cas.

Auldbrig

Doonside Ho.

Martnaham Lo.

Mu

ACKNOWLEDGEMENTS

BOOK ILLUSTRATION

Brigid Collins practices as an artist and illustrator and is a lecturer at
Duncan of Jordanstone College of Art, a faculty of The University of
Dundee, in Scotland. She creates paintings and assemblages in 2 and 3D,
often commissioned by design agencies, publishers and art buyers,
nationally and internationally. In 2004, she was commissioned by
The University of Dundee to create artworks for 'Room to Rhyme', an
illustrated publication of a speech given by the Irish poet and Nobel
Laureate, Seamus Heaney. Passionate in her desire to forge relationships
between images and words, particularly poetry, which is a constant
source of inspiration, she often collaborates with writers and poets
and also exhibits widely.

www.scottishillustrators.com

This book has been made possible by the William Harvey Trust, Dundee,
Homecoming Scotland, the College of Arts and Social Sciences,
University of Dundee and External Relations, University of Dundee.

We would like to thank Dundee Rep for their support.

We would also like to thank Joan Concannon, University of Dundee.

For A' That was conceived, created and edited by Kirsty Gunn and Anna Day.

Anna Day is Director of the Dundee Literary Festival and of Winter Words,
Pitlochry. She also works for Dundee University Press, the Dundee
International Book Prize, Dundee Literary Salons and LiteraryDundee,
an umbrella website and home for all the literary activities in the city.

To find out more go to www.literarydundee.co.uk

For permission to reproduce images in their collection, the editors
would like to thank City of Dundee Archives, Central Library,
Edinburgh Central Library and Dumfries Museum.

Burns extracts from the James Kinsley Edition.

ISBN 9781 84586 0875